THE MODEL BAKERY COOKBOOK

THE

MODEL BAKERY

COOKBOOK

꧁ ⸱ ꧂

75 FAVORITE RECIPES *from the*
BELOVED NAPA VALLEY BAKERY

KAREN MITCHELL *and*
SARAH MITCHELL HANSEN
with **RICK RODGERS**

Photographs by
FRANKIE FRANKENY

CHRONICLE BOOKS
SAN FRANCISCO

Library of Congress Cataloging–in–Publication Data available.

ISBN 978-1-4521-1383-8

Manufactured in China

Designed by Alice Chau
Typesetting by Helen Lee

10 9 8 7 6 5 4 3 2

Chronicle Books LLC
680 Second Street
San Francisco, California 94107
www.chroniclebooks.com

CONTENTS

INTRODUCTION

The year was 1984, and I was a young, naive, and determined self-taught chef. I was operating a small but thriving catering business, hidden in a back alley behind Main Street in the center of the small town of St. Helena, in the heart of California's best-known wine region. My landlord, who was both a good friend and my attorney, also owned the building that housed the town bakery. I had long dreamed of owning the St. Helena Bakery, which was operated by a European family. The location, the building, the interior space, and the ovens were perfectly suited to my idealistic aspirations.

When the building became available, my husband, John, and I immediately decided to rent it. I was elated, even though months of hard work lay ahead. I never doubted that we could renovate the facility, develop a new product line, and make a successful venture out of this wonderful old building. The premises had been vacated, and nearly all the equipment had been removed. The only things remaining were two brick ovens built into the walls during the 1920s. Most of the old brick hearth ovens in bakeries in California (and elsewhere in the United States) had already disappeared, replaced with electric convection ovens. I had always coveted those beautiful brick hearth ovens, which were partly baking tools and partly antiques.

The bakery products available in the Napa Valley in the early 1980s were San Francisco sourdough breads, often made from mixes. There were almost no artisan breads. Having traveled throughout Europe, I had fallen in love with European baking and was determined to bring European artisan baking techniques to the Napa Valley—using those wonderful brick ovens. I longed to create naturally fermented sourdoughs and wonderful European-style croissants and pastries. At the time, I had no idea how big the project would become. I never stopped to realize that I now had the only bakery in the entire upper Napa Valley, nor did I dream that the bakery might grow into what it is today.

The hundred-year-old brick building was charming in an old-world way, with tiled windows, high ceilings, and even skylights. Our plan was to keep the historical details intact and create an environment that had the feeling of a 1930s café. At the same time,

we had to make the bakery functional and wanted to maintain an open feeling by keeping the two areas, retail and production, visible from the entry all the way to the back door.

Starting a bakery from the bottom up is an expensive and demanding endeavor. Bakery equipment is unique and twice as costly as basic restaurant machinery. I was fortunate that my husband is a building contractor with an MBA, because without his direction, I never could have taken on the renovation. John and his crew constructed the worktables, installed refrigeration and plumbing, updated the electrical system, built the bread displays and cabinetry, and did all the painting. Everything seemed to fall into place, except for one major hurdle—we had no idea how to fire and operate the bakery's old brick ovens, and we had to learn by trial and error.

Each oven was formidable—approximately 18 ft/5.5 m wide, 14 ft/4.3 m deep, and 16 in/40.5 cm high. The bricks on the floor were set in a bed of sand, and the oven ceiling was mortared into an arch. The ovens were heated by huge natural-gas "guns" attached to the walls on a swivel of galvanized pipe. Like the ovens, the gas guns with blower fans were probably manufactured in the 1920s. To light an oven, the gas guns were inserted into the mouth of the oven through a steel door. As the gas valve was opened and the blowers forced air in, the mixture was ignited by a propane torch. At full force, the guns resembled giant flamethrowers and made a deep growling noise that shook the windows all the way to the front of the building. The heat was aimed alternately at the center and then to the left and right sides of each oven to heat the brick surfaces evenly.

It was an enormous challenge to figure out the correct firing techniques and the oven temperatures. Our first tries were almost comical, and we had occasional mishaps, such as the time when a flash of flame caught John's sweater on fire.

We learned that the specially designed heat sink—a 3-ft-/1-m-deep layer of solid dry sand—in the attic directly above the ovens could hold most of the oven heat from day to day. It was so effective that

an oven fully heated to a baking temperature of around 600°F/ 315°C would take three weeks to cool down to 90°F/32°C. Bringing the ovens up to baking temperature took one to two hours. If we baked right away, everything burned on the bottom. As we continued to experiment, we discovered that we could do our baking in stages without having to refire the oven.

First, the sourdough breads would go in, and the steam heat, at full strength, would allow the loaves to rise. The steam, produced from a boiler connected directly to the original pipes in the oven walls, would come billowing out of the mouth of the oven, almost like a fire-breathing dragon. After perhaps five minutes, the steam would be shut off, and the ovens would revert to dry heat, which crisped the crusts of the bread. The aromas were incredible. After the first bake, as the ovens cooled slightly, we could continue with French loaves and finally with our more delicate, thin-crusted loaves. Later in the shift, we would refire the ovens and bake our morning pastries, muffins, and scones. In a modern bakery, the power would be left on all night to heat the electric ovens. Our method was more economical—natural gas being much cheaper than electricity—and the products were exceptional.

During the six months of renovation and experimentation with the brick ovens, I befriended Pascal, a French baker who had worked in a small bakery in southern France from his apprenticeship at age fourteen until he reached the master baker level in his late twenties. He was a huge source of knowledge and practical experience, and all his baking had been done in ovens similar to ours. I hired him, and we began to develop our line of baked goods.

We were thrilled to open the doors just before Thanksgiving of 1984. The interior of the retail area was like that of a small bakery in the countryside of Provence. The walls were golden mustard and the wooden trim a deep forest green, colors taken from the ceramic tiles in the windows (and also from the local wild mustard fields and verdant vineyards). When customers walked in the door, they saw the baked goods displayed in wicker baskets and glass-front wood cabinets. Initially we offered simple sweet French and sourdough breads and a couple of flavored breads, along with some pastries and cookies. A stand-up counter along one wall was for coffee and tea service.

All along, my goal was to provide the area with the kind of small-town bakery that was fast disappearing, a place where kids would stop by on the way home from school for a cookie, or where a customer could pick up a delicious birthday cake at a moment's notice. There was a time when every community had a bakery like this, but the convenience of buying baked goods (usually of dubious quality) at a supermarket had lured customers away, and many of these establishments closed. I believed that if our food proved to be as good as I wanted it to be, customers wouldn't be able to resist.

How the bakery got its name is a complete coincidence. One day during construction, a good friend who had grown up in St. Helena stopped by to check our progress. As he walked through the bakery, he mumbled something like "Ah . . . the Model Bakery." We asked him what he meant. He explained that the bakery was known as the Model Bakery during his childhood in the 1930s. We adopted the name instantly.

In the first years we owned the bakery we were still catering, and many of our first customers were the local vintners who hired us to cater events. In this way we became familiar with the new, burgeoning wineries and the people behind them. We experimented with recipes a lot in those days, and we learned by doing. In fact, many people in the town, including Isabel Mondavi (Michael Mondavi's wife and a member of the famous winemaking family), joined us in baking and cooking all kinds of recipes as we found our way.

Every year the Robert Mondavi Winery organized the Great Chefs of France, during which the world's most famous chefs gathered to teach classes to their fans. Some of these superstars included Julia Child, Gaston Lenôtre, Michel Guérard, Paul Prudhomme, Jacques Pépin, and Alain Chapel. The Mondavis hired us to cater the breakfast, and I got to attend the classes in return. I would get up at 5:00 A.M., bake off the croissants, squeeze orange juice, deliver the goods, and then run home to change and return in time for classes. Being around these chefs, who represented a level of professionalism that would be the dream of any young baker, helped expand my view of what was possible with my little bakery. Our reputation grew, and we had a lot of chefs stopping by, including Julia (who signed my first edition of *Mastering the Art of French Cooking*). One time, a couple came in the back door to check us out. They were Wolfgang Puck and beloved dessert cookbook author Maida Heatter. "We hear you are doing a great job," Wolfgang said. It was music to my ears.

We were also in on the ground floor of another well-known local event. Auction Napa Valley started in the 1980s and was organized by wine country dynamo Molly Chappellet to promote local wineries and as a benefit for the region's hospitals. It has become one of the largest charity events in the country, and last year it had more than two thousand attendees and raised seven million dollars. It began as a lunch at Meadowood, our area's top golf course and a top-notch country hotel, cooked by Bay Area celebrity chef Narsai David. For that first meal for three hundred guests, we filled beautiful grapevine baskets with fresh pâtés, salads, and sweets. We've been a part of the auction every year since.

Charitable giving is a huge part of our mission, and we donate to many local causes. Being part of the community is such an important part of what we do, whether we're supplying bread for school lunches or making iced cookies in the shape of fire hydrants for the fire department. I've seen many kids grow up—I've baked wedding cakes for the same young women for whom I used to bake birthday cakes. We now hire externs from the nearby Culinary Institute of America at Greystone, who come work with us while earning their degrees. Being part of the community, learning, and giving back have been among the great joys of running the bakery. They are the reasons I have been able to maintain my passion for it.

HOW IT ALL BEGAN

I am often asked how I got started in the food business. The easiest answer is that cooking has been in my blood since childhood.

I grew up in Portland, Oregon, in a family of good cooks of Norwegian descent. My mother and grandmothers were among the best cooks of their time. All of our food was made from scratch. We grew our own vegetables and fruits, and my father was a serious outdoorsman who fished and hunted. My father's Auntie Emma operated a prestigious dining room in Portland called Berg's Chalet, an old brick mansion turned into a restaurant, where James Beard often dined when he was in town (Beard was an Oregonian). As young girls, my sister and I would visit for family celebrations and end up in the kitchen watching the cooks fry chicken and steaks. We especially liked being allowed to make our own ice-cream sundaes. Emma was a skilled baker. Her buttermilk cake with strawberry cream frosting was featured in the restaurant, and it was the centerpiece of every Fourth of July picnic. I saved her old recipes and continue to use them in my bakery.

Fruit was so abundant in Oregon that it seemed as if everyone was an expert at making pies. On my mother's side, my Aunt Lou was the town baker in Enterprise, Oregon. She had a baking kitchen in the back of her home, where she produced all the pies for the general store (owned by her sister), the local café, and the lumber mill. In those days, pie was served at every meal, including breakfast. My sister and I would sit on tall stools in her kitchen and watch her work. Sometimes she would let us peel fruit or sift flour. She made little pies for us as a treat. Little did I know that I would someday be doing the same with my own daughter, Sarah.

When I attended Willamette University in Salem, Oregon, I organized Sunday night dinners at our sorority, where I was house manager. It was the cook's night off and, rather than serve cold cuts, I decided we would have theme dinners, such as Italian feasts and French picnics. Back then, in the mid-1960s, the shopping possibilities were slim, but the sorority girls adored the dinners, and I began to enjoy feeding my friends.

After marrying and moving around the country with John, my Marine Corps pilot husband, I was exposed to many different culinary flavors. We lived in Pensacola, Florida, where I happily ate oysters and Gulf shrimp. We moved to Southern California and I got to know Mexican food. When I finished graduate school in Los Angeles, we decided to travel before settling down. After selling most of our belongings, we flew to Germany, where we bought a new VW bus. Thus began a two-year odyssey: Europe on five dollars a day.

As we went from country to country, we explored the local street markets, bakeries, pubs, and wine bars. We cooked many of our meals in the bus, so I shopped and experimented with food, and became more and more enamored with European ways. We headed first to Scandinavia, where my ancestors had lived, and then we went south to Paris, which was to become perhaps our favorite place in the world. We experienced the thrill of buying baguettes just out of the oven and savoring buttery croissants and brioches in the morning. The pastries were exquisite. There was nothing like this at home. How could I ever eat soft, squishy American bread again? Naturally, I fell in love with real Italian food as well. I scoured the markets, bakeries, and pizzerias for new tastes and collected ideas for the growing list of foods I wanted to make when I got back to the States. While in the British Isles, I discovered wonderful cheeses, dark breads, smoked salmon, and scones. I wanted to bring these new friends home with me.

When we returned after our trip around the world, we were changed people, and it was difficult to imagine working in serious jobs in a city. After a few false starts, we moved to the Napa Valley. In the early 1970s, the wine business was just starting to expand. New wineries were being built, and existing wineries were upgrading their vineyards. The focus was on European-style winemaking. The old-world influence on wine started to trickle down to the style of food served in the Napa Valley. More restaurants were opening that offered sophisticated, European-inspired food.

My husband, a dedicated wine enthusiast, worked the crush at Burgess Cellars and began to meet people in the Valley. In 1975, we encountered two European friends who were running a small French-style bistro in Calistoga. After many shared meals, they asked me to help them cook for special parties. The next spring we helped them open a restaurant in St. Helena called La Belle Hélène. I cooked lunches and they cooked dinners. It was a daunting experience for someone with no restaurant experience. I worked from early morning through the afternoon, while John watched our new baby. Then he went to work nights at a winery.

Bitten seriously by the restaurant life, I cooked with friends for various winery clients I met while at La Belle. The rapid growth of wineries had generated a big demand for entertaining, but there were no high-end restaurants or markets in the Napa Valley. I decided to open a commercial kitchen in St. Helena and put all our friends to work. We had the most sophisticated servers anywhere. The business was hectic and exciting and lucrative. I cooked lunch for Joseph Phelps and his staff every Tuesday, when they would entertain restaurateurs and wine writers. My first guests were Alice Waters and Jeremiah Tower from Chez Panisse. I was petrified but received compliments from everyone.

A FAMILY BAKERY

Two decades after the Model Bakery opened, my daughter, Sarah, who had gone to work in the corporate world, realized that she missed life in the wine country. She decided to move back to Napa and join the bakery business. She and her fiancé, Chris, worked together at the bakery for a year, until he was lured away by the wine industry. After a grand wedding and honeymoon, Sarah took on more responsibilities at the bakery.

The introduction of young talent and their new marketing ideas enabled us to take the bakery to a whole new level. There was a great demand from local restaurants and hotels for us to supply their baking needs, but the brick ovens in St. Helena could not accommodate the volume. We had reached capacity in both oven space and storage space, and by 2007 we clearly needed a bigger and more up-to-date facility. The old brick ovens were wearing down, especially the steam machine system—essential for crusty

bread—with its corroded and inaccessible piping in the walls. We juggled and coped with our limited work space.

In 2007, we were approached by a local developer planning a food hall in downtown Napa, called Oxbow Public Market, a project from the same team that started the Ferry Building Marketplace in San Francisco. He was looking for local food businesses to come together under one roof and offer the finest products in the Napa Valley. Our problem was space—we needed at least 2,000 square feet/186 square metres to set up a production bakery.

The solution was to move the bread operation to a facility in Napa with new ovens and mixing equipment. We contacted the San Francisco Baking Institute and planned a complete bakery. The building we chose was formerly an auto-tire store. We hired Howard Backen, a well-known local architect, to transform it into a modern bakery. Here we go again, I thought—we had to remodel the entire facility. In it we installed state-of-the-art brick deck ovens from Italy. The project took almost one year from design to opening.

In the middle of the project, our head baker informed us he was going to move closer to his family in Tennessee. My daughter, ever the optimist, found an experienced *boulanger* in Lyon, France (through the Internet, we were taking a big chance!). We brought him to California with his wife and new baby and incorporated his experience and skills into our new baking operation. That was a nerve-wracking time, but through the process, we found several other talented bread bakers who were as excited as we were to open our bakery in the Oxbow Public Market in the winter of 2008.

We operate around the clock, seven days a week, with a staff of more than fifty. Our baking team is truly a sight to behold. (Actually it is two teams, as we do the sweet pastries in St. Helena, and the yeasted breads in Napa.) They are dedicated to their work and proud of what they accomplish each day. Our delivery truck makes two or three trips daily from St. Helena to Napa and back.

Our baked goods are intentionally simple, with familiar old-fashioned flavors. "Homespun" is another way to describe their comforting taste and visual appeal. I have amassed a gold mine of recipes. They began as simple working recipes and have been refined and improved over the years. We started with small-kitchen methods and worked carefully to develop them for a commercial scale. For this cookbook, we went backward, reducing commercial formulas to the small scale we began with more than thirty years ago so that they can be reproduced successfully in the home kitchen.

I am always pleased when customers remark, "This is the best cookie I've ever eaten," because their palates show how hard we've worked on refining our recipes. The bakery's Chocolate Rads (page 173), English Muffins (page 35), and Almond Macaroons (page 176) are items that people come miles to enjoy, even though they could buy similar items elsewhere. Occasionally, we will give a nod to more contemporary flavors, as we do with our Chocolate and Caramel Tartlets with Fleur de Sel (page 150). The book starts with an explanation of important ingredients, equipment, and baking techniques—without going into excruciating detail—because they are used again and again. Once you understand these basics, you are on your way to being a great baker.

This book is a collection of my most treasured recipes. It is also the story of our bakery, which is intertwined with the vibrant culinary history of the Napa Valley.

Karen Mitchell
ST. HELENA, CALIFORNIA

INGREDIENTS

Any baker will tell you that fine baking depends on top-notch ingredients. Model Bakery is located in a world-famous agricultural region, and we have great local sources for dairy products, eggs (some come from our pet chickens), and produce. While our flour comes from Utah, its distributor is only a short drive away, and we have a long-standing relationship with them. Here are some notes on the ingredients we use every day. Search out the best in your area, and you will be well on your way to great baking.

CHOCOLATE AND COCOA

You will see a lot of potentially confusing information on chocolate labels. Unsweetened is self-explanatory. According to the U.S. Department of Agriculture (USDA), semisweet and bittersweet chocolate are in the same category, with anywhere from 35 to 88 percent cacao (pure ground cacao beans). The remaining ingredients in chocolate are sweetener (usually sugar), vanilla flavoring (not always pure vanilla and often artificial vanillin), and lecithin, an emulsifier. The higher the cacao content, the more bitter the chocolate.

While some people like bittersweet chocolate with a high cacao content, we take a middle-of-the-road approach for our everyday baking. Our chocolate of choice is Guittard French Vanilla, which has a cacao content of 54 percent. It isn't sold in bars, but some markets in the Bay Area sell it in bulk as chunks. (Guittard is based in Burlingame, California, and has been in operation since 1868.) Any semisweet chocolate with similar cacao content, such as Lindt Excellence Sweet Dark or Callebaut Semisweet, will do very well.

CHOCOLATE CHIPS. There are a lot of good chocolate chips out there, so just use your favorite brand. We like Guittard semisweet chocolate chips. When buying white chocolate chips for the White Chocolate Chip and Hazelnut Cookies (page 182), look carefully at the ingredients, as the main fat should be cocoa butter. Skip brands that use coconut oil or palm oil.

COCOA. Essentially ground cacao beans, natural cocoa powder is very acidic. It needs to be neutralized by including an alkali (usually baking soda) in the batter. The reaction between the acid and alkali make carbon dioxide, which helps the batter rise. Hershey's, in the brown container, is a widely available brand of natural cocoa powder; Scharffen Berger is a fine boutique product. Most of our recipes use natural cocoa.

In the nineteenth century, a Dutch chocolatier developed a process to alkalize the cocoa, thereby reducing its acidity, and at the same time changing its color to a reddish brown. This is called Dutch-process or alkalized cocoa. It is not interchangeable with natural cocoa. It may not be clear from the label if the cocoa is Dutched or alkalized, so look for alkali on the ingredients list.

DAIRY PRODUCTS

Always use whole-fat dairy products in your recipes so you don't throw off the fat balance and risk a flop. This is especially true for sour cream, milk, and cream cheese (we prefer Philadelphia brand as its flavor and texture are perfect for baking). Heavy cream and whipping cream are interchangeable, but just be sure the whipping cream isn't flavored or stabilized.

EGGS

As a leavening, emulsifier, binder, and provider of moisture and flavor, eggs play many roles in baking. We use whole eggs most often, but sometimes the eggs are separated and the whites are beaten alone and folded into the batter to incorporate air.

Use large grade A eggs, and make sure they are not cracked. Size may not seem like much of an issue, but if your recipe calls for a lot of eggs, there is a big difference between the volume of six jumbo eggs and six large eggs.

THE MODEL BAKERY COOKBOOK

Store eggs in their carton in the refrigerator, and not the egg compartment on the door, which can be too warm for efficient chilling. However, eggs have the most elasticity and emulsifying properties when at room temperature. (If you add cold eggs to room-temperature creamed butter and sugar, the mixture may curdle because of the discrepancy in temperature between the ingredients.) Let the eggs stand at room temperature for 30 minutes before using, or place the eggs in their shells in a bowl of warm tap water and let them stand for 5 minutes to lose their chill. To bring reserved egg whites to room temperature, put the whites in a heat-proof bowl and let the bowl stand in a large bowl of warm tap water, stirring the egg whites occasionally, just until they lose their chill, about 5 minutes.

FATS

Fat gives baked goods tenderness, moisture, and, in most cases, flavor. It comes from both animal and vegetable sources.

BUTTER. Beloved by bakers (and pastry eaters) for its unsurpassable flavor, unsalted butter allows the baker to control the amount of salt in the recipe. Use grade AA or A butter, which has the butterfat content (about 80 percent) and moisture for good elasticity during creaming and the best flavor. In our croissant dough, we use high-butterfat butter (more than 83 percent), which is usually labeled European-style butter. Croissant dough is rolled out repeatedly and needs the flexibility provided by the extra butterfat. Plugrá is a well-distributed high-butterfat butter, but you may find a local producer.

VEGETABLE OIL. You can use any kind of oil with a light body and neutral flavor: canola, corn, safflower, or a generic vegetable oil blend.

VEGETABLE SHORTENING. Made from solidified vegetable oil, it makes our pastry dough extra-flaky. Until recently the oil was hydrogenated to solidify it, a process that formed trans fats, which are known to have adverse health effects. Shortening has been reformulated and is no longer hydrogenated.

FLOUR

Wheat flour is the most important ingredient in baking, as it determines the texture of the final product. You may think of flour as a carbohydrate, and you would be correct, but it also contains two proteins, gliadin and glutenin, that are responsible for the texture variations. When these two are moistened with water or other liquids, they combine to form gluten and create an invisible matrix, which traps the carbon dioxide formed by the leavening in the dough. The higher the protein content of the flour, the more potential for gluten, which makes baked goods chewy but can also make them tough.

Wheat flour is often designated by the variety of wheat (soft or hard, a reference to its potential finished texture after baking) or growing season (spring or winter, as the harshness of the season affects the amount of protein in the wheat). Some flours are chemically bleached to improve their shelf life. We prefer unbleached flour for its superior flavor and lack of unnecessary additives.

We buy our flour from Keith Giusto Bakery Supply, in nearby Petaluma, which distributes Central Milling flour from Utah. (The Giusto family has been the premier flour supplier to the Bay Area for generations.) Keith doesn't offer mail order, but some Whole Foods Markets in Northern California carry Central Milling flours as their proprietary brand or offer them in bulk. Buy organic flour whenever possible, as its flavor is superior. We recommend King Arthur flour, which is available throughout the country.

Note that we measure flour by the dip-and-sweep method (see page 29).

BREAD FLOUR. As its name implies, this unbleached flour with a high protein content is best reserved for yeasted goods. Bread dough made with bread flour has a high gluten content; it can withstand vigorous kneading as well as rising (from the yeast's carbon dioxide). Bromated bread flour has been treated with potassium bromate, a possible carcinogen, and it should be avoided. Most producers now use ascorbic acid as a substitute for the potassium bromate as it has similar properties. We used King Arthur bread flour for testing recipes. It has no additives and a slightly higher protein content than most national brands.

CAKE FLOUR. A soft-wheat flour with low protein (and therefore low gluten) content, it makes tender cakes. Bleached cake flour, under the brand names Softasilk and Swans Down, is available at every supermarket. If you can find it, King Arthur's unbleached cake flour is a very good product. Do not use self-rising cake flour, which includes leavening. Check the label carefully to be sure you are buying regular cake flour.

RYE FLOUR. Milled from whole rye kernels, rye flour should be stored in the refrigerator so it doesn't turn rancid. We use it in our Wild Yeast Grape Starter (page 56) because it ferments more readily than wheat flour.

SEMOLINA. Semolina is durum wheat ground to a gritty, sandy texture. Think of it as cornmeal, rather than flour (although it is often incorrectly labeled semolina flour). While it can be used to make bread (and pasta), we sprinkle it on bread peels to make a slippery surface for sliding bread off the peel and into the oven.

UNBLEACHED ALL-PURPOSE FLOUR. All-purpose flour means that it will work well in a variety of baked goods, from cookies to pies. Standard all-purpose flour, made from a combination of soft and hard flours, is bleached, a process that reduces the protein. We prefer unbleached all-purpose, which has a relatively high protein count. The butter and sugar act as tenderizers to keep the baked goods from getting too chewy. We used King Arthur all-purpose flour to test many of the recipes in this book.

WHOLE-WHEAT FLOUR. Milled from the entire kernel, including the bran and germ, this is a high-protein flour that makes a very sturdy bread. In fact, most bakers add some white flour to whole-wheat dough to keep the baked bread from being too tough. Store whole-wheat flour in the refrigerator, as the fat in the bran and germ makes it turn rancid more quickly than white flour.

LEAVENINGS

When a dough or batter is beaten (especially when creaming butter and sugar for cakes and cookies), tiny air bubbles are formed. Leavenings are added to create carbon dioxide, which makes these bubbles expand during baking so the product rises and becomes lighter. The three most common leavenings are baking powder, baking soda, and yeast.

BAKING POWDER. This leavening is made from a combination of alkaline baking soda and acidic cream of tartar, and when moistened, it forms carbon dioxide. Unlike baking soda alone, it does not need additional acidic ingredients to activate.

BAKING SODA. Also known as bicarbonate of soda, this alkaline ingredient must be used with acidic ingredients (such as natural cocoa, brown sugar, buttermilk, vinegar, or molasses) to produce the chemical reaction that forms carbon dioxide. If you have ever mixed baking soda with vinegar for a science experiment, you can visualize the process.

YEAST. We use only instant yeast. It is also sold as quick-rising or bread-machine yeast. It has many advantages over the familiar active dry yeast and compressed fresh yeast. First of all, instant yeast can be mixed with cool water, while active dry needs a temperature of about 110°F/43°C to melt the yeast granules' encapsulations. When a bread dough is made using cool water, the yeast works at a slower pace, and the baked bread's flavor is deeper and more complex. The popularity of this yeast is getting to the point where some supermarkets carry it exclusively and don't even bother with the other varieties anymore. You can buy instant yeast in a strip of three ¼-oz/7-g envelopes or a 4-oz/115-g glass jar. After opening, store the jar in the refrigerator. Do not buy yeast in large quantities unless you are sure you are going to use it up before it expires (there is always a use-by date on the package).

NUTS

Bakers often use nuts to add flavor and crunch to a recipe. For the most part, almonds, walnuts, hazelnuts, and pecans are interchangeable, and you can choose according to your palate. Almonds can be processed by the producer in different ways. Natural almonds retain their brown skin; blanched almonds have had the skins removed. Slivered almonds are cut into elongated strips, and sliced almonds are thin flakes.

For many years, walnuts were the main crop in the Napa Valley. With the high demand for wine grapes, most walnut orchards were converted to vineyards, and walnut production moved north to Lake County. We still use them a lot in our baking. To toast nuts, see page 30.

SALT

Use fine sea salt in baking. Table salt, which is iodized, has additives that some palates can detect. We use flaky, coarse-grained sea salt, such as *fleur de sel de Guérande* or Maldon, for the garnish and flavoring on our Chocolate and Caramel Tartlets with Fleur de Sel (page 150).

SUGAR

In baking, sugar performs as a sweetener and tenderizer and also provides bulk. We prefer the flavor and texture of pure cane sugar to beet sugar; check the package to be sure that you are buying the former.

BROWN SUGAR. Once a by-product of sugar refining (like molasses), brown sugar is usually, these days, granulated sugar sprayed with molasses. (Muscovado sugar is brown sugar manufactured by the traditional method, and while it is pricey, some bakers love it.) Whether brown sugar is light or dark merely depends on how much molasses is added. They are interchangeable, although dark brown sugar does make darker baked goods. Moist in texture, brown sugar is always measured by packing it firmly into the measuring cup and leveling the top, or by weight. If your brown sugar is lumpy, rub it through a coarse-mesh sieve before using. Store brown sugar in an airtight container to keep it from drying out and hardening.

CONFECTIONERS' SUGAR. Also called powdered sugar, confectioners' sugar is mainly used as an ingredient in frosting and as a garnish for baked goods. It should be stored in an airtight container, as it can absorb humidity and clump. Confectioners' sugar is usually sifted before using to ensure a smooth texture.

GRANULATED SUGAR. Refined to a pristine white color, this sugar has moderately sized crystals that blend well with butter.

LIGHT CORN SYRUP. This clear syrup discourages crystallization in boiled syrups. It also makes ganache glossy and gives it a softer texture. If you wish, substitute British golden syrup, available at specialty stores and many supermarkets, which is processed from cane syrup, not corn.

MOLASSES. A by-product of sugar refining, molasses is a dark brown syrup with a strong flavor. Various brands have different labels to indicate the flavor strength. You can use light, dark, or unsulfured molasses, but blackstrap molasses, made from the final round of processing, is too bitter.

SANDING SUGAR. This coarse-grained sugar is used as a decoration on cookies. We call it "big sugar" at the bakery.

VANILLA

Vanilla is an essential flavoring. It is always expensive because the flowers must be pollinated by hand (and there is only one day a year that the flowers open wide enough for the workers to reach the stamens and pistils), and vanilla beans are grown in only a few tropical regions. Pure vanilla extract is best, and let's not even discuss artificial vanilla flavoring. We love Singing Dog Vanilla (see Resources, page 199), which has an amazingly full flavor and is made from beans harvested by small family farms in tropical regions.

EQUIPMENT

Have you ever heard someone say, "I'm a good cook, but I can't bake"? We have. Upon further investigation, we often find that the person has terrible baking equipment—warped, flimsy baking sheets; an insufficient number of measuring cups (too many people use a single glass cup for measuring everything, which is just wrong); an ancient hand mixer (when they own a mixer at all); and foil pie pans that buckle on the way to the oven. Supply your kitchen well, and prime yourself for baking success.

APPLIANCES

ELECTRIC HAND MIXER. This is a very handy appliance when you want to whip a serving or two of cream or when the stand mixer is already in use. Some of them are strong enough to do just about anything a stand mixer can do, except knead bread.

FOOD PROCESSOR. A food processor makes short work of chopping nuts and other kitchen chores, and there are some jobs that almost require it. An example is processing the almond paste and sugar for our Almond Macaroons (page 176)—it can be done in batches in a blender, but it is quicker to do it in a single batch in the larger work bowl of the food processor.

OVEN. Allow at least 15 minutes for the oven to preheat for regular baking, and at least 30 minutes for it to reach the high temperature required for baking artisan bread. A convection oven has a fan that circulates the hot air and helps food brown more easily. We never use one. It's not that we don't recommend it; we just don't use them in our home kitchens. If you want to use a convection oven, follow the manufacturer's instructions. In general, reduce the oven temperature in a standard recipe by 25°F/15°C, reduce the cooking time by about one-third, and use the recipe's visual and tactile tests to check for doneness.

STAND MIXER. We don't know any professional baker or serious home baker who doesn't own a heavy-duty stand mixer. It is a great laborsaving machine as well as a time-saver because it frees your hands to do something else while the machine is creaming butter, whipping cream, or kneading bread dough. (That does not mean that you don't have to pay attention to the mixing.) In short, if you love baking, get a stand mixer. We have supplied instructions for making the recipes with a spoon or hand mixer whenever possible, but once you experience the efficiency of a stand mixer, you will never go back. Stand mixers are an investment. Keep an eye out for sales or coupons, and you can score a bargain. (We gave this advice recently to a customer who wanted a stand mixer but balked at the price. She bought a mixer with a coupon at a department store, and she has been thanking us ever since. She went from never baking to baking all the time. Point taken?)

A model with a 5½-qt/5.2-L bowl has the most versatility. Some models have 5-qt/4.7-L bowls, and while 2 cups/480 ml doesn't seem like much of a difference, it will be if you try to double a buttercream recipe.

The paddle-shaped attachment for most stand mixer models isn't too efficient, as it doesn't reach the sides and bottom of the bowl, so you have to stop the mixer often to scrape it down. BeaterBlade, an after-purchase product replacement for the paddle, does a great job of mixing and scraping at the same time.

BAKING PANS

Professional bakers buy equipment for efficiency, not looks. Most of our pans look pretty beat up from years of use, but that is exactly why we keep them—we know they work. Most of our baking pans are made from heavy-gauge aluminum with a dull patina. This material soaks up the oven heat and promotes even browning. Shiny metal pans reflect the heat.

CAKE PANS AND BAKING PANS. For our layer cakes, we use three cake pans, each 8 in/20 cm in diameter and 2 in/5 cm deep. If you are going to make the wedding cake on page 128, you will need a single 6-in/15-cm pan with the same depth, too. Heavy-gauge aluminum pans, without a nonstick coating, are our first choice. These pans need to be buttered and floured before adding the batter. The most useful baking pan size is 13 by 9 by 2 in/33 by 23 by 5 cm.

FLUTED TUBE PANS. Most people call these Bundt pans, but Bundt is a trademark. You could also use a kugelhopf pan, as long as the capacity is 12 cups/2.8 L. Always butter and flour the pan, even if it's nonstick.

HALF-SHEET PANS. A bakery can never have enough of these pans, which are all-purpose baking sheets. Measuring 18 by 13 by 1 in/ 46 by 33 by 2.5 cm, they are sturdy and hold up year after year. (A full sheet pan, which will not fit into home ovens, is 26 in/66 cm long.) We also like quarter-sheet pans, which measure 13 by 9 by 1 in/ 33 by 23 by 2.5 cm, and are perfect for when you only need to toast a small amount of nuts or seeds. We use the generic term "large rimmed baking sheet" in some recipes, but your baking is sure to improve if you use professional half-sheet pans.

The thin and shiny cookie sheets that many home bakers have encourage burned cookie bottoms. Because they are often rimless, they are hard to hold. We don't use them. Nor do we recommend insulated double-thick cookie sheets—the extra air discourages browning, often at the expense of caramelized flavor.

LOAF PANS. Bread pans are available in three basic sizes. To be sure that we get plenty of slices out of each loaf, we use 9-by-5-by-3-in/23-by-12-by-7.5-cm loaf pans.

MUFFIN PANS. Use standard muffin cups with about a ½-cup/ 120-ml capacity. Each cup measures about 2¾ in/7 cm across and is about 1½ in/4 cm deep.

PIE PANS. We like standard pie pans, 9 in/23 cm in diameter and 1½ in/4 cm deep, made from heavy-duty aluminum or Pyrex. Beware of deeper pans made from ceramic; they may look attractive, but you will not have enough filling or pie dough to fill them.

TARTLET PANS. We often make tartlets for individual servings in 5-in-/12-cm-diameter pans with removable bottoms.

TART PANS. These metal, two-piece pans have removable bottoms, so a tart can be easily lifted from the pan for easy slicing. Do not use one-piece ceramic pans.

UTENSILS AND OTHER ESSENTIALS

BAKER'S PEEL. This is a wide flat paddle used to move bread into and out of the oven.

BAKING STONE. A necessity for baking artisan breads, the stone provides a very hot, flat surface, which encourages the formation of a crisp crust. Store the stone in the oven, and remove it when you need the oven for baked goods other than breads. It will get stained with use, but don't worry about it.

BENCH SCRAPER. This square metal tool will scrape the work surface clean of dough remnants. You can also use it to cut dough into pieces.

BOWLS. Stainless-steel bowls are the most useful for baking because they are sturdy and heat-proof, an important consideration when you need a large bowl to melt chocolate over hot water. A large ceramic or glass bowl provides the perfect insulated container for fermenting yeasted dough. Rubber or plastic bowls are not recommended, as they retain the flavor and aroma of the dough.

BOWL SCRAPER. This is a flexible, curved utensil that lets the baker scrape out every bit of batter from a mixing bowl.

CARDBOARD CAKE ROUNDS. These sturdy rounds, made from white corrugated cardboard, support cake layers and make it easy to transport the cake.

KITCHEN SCALE. Battery-operated scales are compact, inexpensive, and highly accurate. The scale should toggle easily between metric and U.S. or imperial weights, and have a capacity of at least 10 lb/4.5 kg. Spring scales aren't nearly as accurate and take up more room on the counter. Besides weighing dough, we use scales to distribute equal amounts of batter into cake pans so each layer is the same size after baking.

MEASURING CUPS, DRY-INGREDIENT. The set of squat cups, designed so the ingredient can be leveled off at the top, come in ¼-cup/60-ml, ⅓-cup/75-ml, ½-cup/120-ml, and 1-cup/ 240-ml capacities. If you do a lot of baking, you will find it convenient to have more than one set. There are also cups with ⅔-cup/165-ml and ¾-cup/180-ml capacities, but they are easy to confuse with the others and aren't useful in the long run.

MEASURING CUPS, LIQUID-INGREDIENT. These are made of transparent glass or plastic so you can read the measurement. The most useful sizes are 1 cup/240 ml and 2 cup/480 ml, but the 4-cup/960-ml size is helpful for some large-batch recipes. Most of them provide both metric and U.S. or imperial measurements.

PARCHMENT PAPER. We go through stacks of parchment paper every day, because we line our aluminum half-sheet and cake pans with it to make them nonstick. Look for flat, unrolled parchment paper at kitchen suppliers. If using the rolled paper, lightly butter the pan first to help adhere the curled paper to the pan. Precut parchment rounds for lining cake pans are real time-savers because they spare you the trouble of trimming rectangular paper to size. We don't use silicone baking pads, which some bakers substitute for parchment, because they insulate the baking sheets and inhibit some of our baked goods from browning.

PASTRY BAGS AND TIPS. Used to hold icing for decorating, there are two kinds of bags. The traditional silicone-lined cloth bag must be used in conjunction with a pastry tip. If you use this kind of bag, wash it well after each use and let it air dry. Never use it for savory foods, or you could end up with garlic-scented buttercream. Disposable plastic pastry bags can also be used with pastry tips, but in some cases, the pointed end of the plastic pastry bag can work without a tip. To pipe lines, just snip off the tip of the icing-filled bag with scissors to make a 1/16- to 1/8-in-/2- to 3-mm-wide opening.

Metal pastry tips can make icing decorations with a twist of the wrist. You can accomplish a lot with just a few tips. The two main manufacturers are Ateco and Wilton, who identify their tips by number; note that the numbers are not universal. Some small tips must be used in conjunction with a coupler to fit the pastry bag. We prefer tips with wide bases that fit pastry bags without couplers. This is a great convenience—just snip off the end of a plastic pastry bag, slip in the tip, fill, and decorate away. Ateco makes a range of large tips, easily identified with the #8 as the first digit in the size number. A plain round tip with a 3/8-in/1-cm opening and an open star tip with a 3/8-in/1-cm opening (such as Ateco numbers 804 and 824) will let you do a number of simple decorations.

PASTRY BLENDER. Used for cutting chilled fats into pie, biscuit, and scone dough, it has an advantage over fingertips: it won't warm the fats.

PASTRY BRUSHES. While there are silicone brushes on the market now, natural bristle brushes are still best for bakers, as they distribute glazes and the like in thin, even applications.

PIE WEIGHTS. These reusable aluminum or ceramic balls are used to hold a dough in place in a pie or tart pan during baking. Be sure to line the dough first with parchment paper or aluminum foil, so the weights can be easily removed. Dried beans are an alternative to pie weights and can be reused a few times, but they will eventually go rancid.

PLASTIC WRAP. Buy a large, long (about 18-in/46-cm) roll at a warehouse store or restaurant wholesaler. There will be many times (such as when proofing shaped croissants or Danish pastries) when you will need to cover a large surface, and the long rolls are much easier to use than the shorter supermarket-size wrap.

PORTION SCOOPS. We use spring-loaded metal portion scoops so much at the bakery that they sometimes feel like actual extensions of our arms—a kind of baker Edward Scissorhands. Each size is identified by a seemingly cryptic number, which, in the United States, refers to the number of scoops needed to fill a quart/litre. Especially when filling muffin cups, a portion scoop transfers the batter cleanly and neatly from the bowl to the pan, and makes muffins of an equal size. For this job, a number-16 scoop (with a capacity of 1/4 cup/60 ml is truly indispensable.

REAMER. Use this pointed, ridged tool to easily extract juice from citrus fruit.

ROLLING PINS. We are fans of old-fashioned ball-bearing rolling pins, the tool we used when we learned to make pies. Some bakers prefer a tapered French pin or a hard plastic version, and it is their prerogative. A 12-in/30.5-cm pin is fine for rolling out pie dough for a standard pie pan, but for large-batch laminated dough (such as croissant dough), use a heavy pin that is at least 18 in/46 cm long.

SPATULAS, FLEXIBLE. We prefer sturdy, odor-resistant silicone spatulas for scraping down bowls and transferring batters to pans, rather than the more traditional rubber or hard plastic ones.

Silicone spatulas are heat-proof, which makes them useful for stirring foods such as lemon curd during cooking. A large spatula is the one to use for folding batters, a small one comes in handy for reaching into small jars, and a medium spatula can be used for scraping hot mixtures from the sides of a saucepan during cooking.

SPATULAS, METAL ICING. The large offset model is angled to smooth the batter in a cake pan evenly before baking and is also used for icing cakes. It is especially helpful for spreading buttercream on hard-to-reach places, such as the cake's sides. The typical straight metal spatula works, too, but most professional bakers prefer the versatile offset spatula. A small icing spatula can come in handy when working with small cakes and cookies.

THERMOMETERS. An instant-read thermometer is useful for testing the temperature of egg-based foods (such as lemon curd), which will curdle if overcooked. Use a deep-frying or candy thermometer to gauge the temperature of syrup for meringues and buttercream. In a home kitchen, never bake without an oven thermometer to check the temperature. An accurate oven thermostat is very rare. We don't care if you use a spring-operated dial face or an alcohol-loaded glass thermometer; just use one. We admit that at the St. Helena bakery, we have learned to deal with gas-fired ovens that do not have thermostats. (How do we test the oven temperature? We put a piece of paper in the oven and wait to see how long it takes to brown. Is it ideal? No. And do not try it at home.)

TIMER. Always set a timer when baking, but also use visual and tactile tests to check when your baked goods are done. We like a digital multifunction timer that allows you to time more than one item at once.

TURNTABLE, DECORATING. A turntable is very convenient when icing a cake, as the cake can be rotated for easy access.

WHISKS. These are available in a variety of sizes and shapes. For general mixing, use a medium-size whisk with moderately thick wires. For whipping egg whites by hand, use a large balloon whisk, which has more wires to beat air into the whites.

WIRE COOLING RACKS. Baked goods will cool most quickly if placed on wire cooling racks. It is best to have a few large rectangular racks, which are especially useful for cooling lots of cookies at holiday time. Round wire racks are perfect for removing cake layers from their pans.

WIRE SIEVE. We prefer a medium-mesh wire sieve to a sifter for sifting because the sieve is larger and aerates the dry ingredients more quickly than a canister-style sifter. This size sieve is also good for straining the cooked egg bits from pastry cream and lemon curd. Fine-mesh sieves should be reserved for straining seeds from berry purees.

ZESTER. Microplane zesters have small, sharp teeth to remove the zest from citrus fruit.

BASIC TECHNIQUES

When we hear that some people are intimidated by baking, we can't understand their trepidation. Any activity, from cutting a lawn to using a smartphone, is simply a matter of learning and applying a few basics. And, of course, practice makes perfect. At the bakery, we use the same elemental techniques over and over again to create our signature baked goods. Here are the most important ones to master at home.

CREAMING

Many recipes get their main leavening not from baking powder, baking soda, or yeast, but from the invisible bubbles beaten into the butter and sugar during the creaming process. The chemical leavening only increases the size of the bubbles during baking, and does not actually make them.

During creaming, butter temperature is very important. It should be softened at room temperature to a malleable, plastic texture. One of the most common baking mistakes is softening butter too much. If it is soft and squishy, the bubbles won't form and the baked goods won't rise well. Just cut the butter into 1-in/2.5-cm chunks and let stand for 15 minutes or so. (Never soften butter in the microwave.) If you have a stand mixer, you can use chilled butter right from the refrigerator and let the friction created by the paddle attachment in the bowl do some of the softening. An electric hand mixer works well, too. For centuries, butter and sugar were creamed with a wooden spoon in a bowl, and you can still do so, if you allow at least 7 minutes for the procedure and you have a strong arm. Use a visual test for telling when the butter and sugar have been creamed long enough—the mixture should look very pale yellow and have a light, if not truly fluffy, texture, indicating that sufficient air has been incorporated into the mixture.

MEASURING INGREDIENTS

There has been a lot of controversy surrounding the simple act of measuring baking ingredients. People have been baking for years by the American volume system and made perfectly good baked goods. The case for weighing ingredients goes like this: There are too many variables when the flour is measured in a cup, as it settles slightly differently every time. Flour is the ingredient that is most affected by the weather (it soaks up humidity and can be heavier on wet days) and by the way it has been packed in its bag for shipping.

At the bakery, we weigh our ingredients because we are working with huge quantities. At home, Karen usually uses measuring cups because it is how she learned to bake, and she has never had a failure based on how the flour was measured. Sarah, on the other hand, prefers a scale. (Perhaps this is a telling generational difference.) In this book we provide both volume and metric weight measurements, so you can use your preferred method. One very important tip: Stick with one measuring system through the recipe, and do not mix them.

When measuring flour for the recipes in this book, we used the dip-and-sweep method because it is the method that most home bakers seem to prefer. To measure by this method, dip the cup into the bag or container so the flour is overflowing, and sweep off the excess flour with a knife so it is level with the rim of the cup. If you are an adamant spoon-and-sweep adherent, meaning you lightly spoon flour into a cup (what a mess) before leveling, your flour could weigh less than ours. Check the weight of your flour against the metric weight we provide, or subtract 1 Tbsp of flour per 1 cup.

MELTING CHOCOLATE

To melt chocolate, coarsely chop the chocolate with a large knife. Do not chop chocolate in a food processor, as the friction can cause premature melting. Put the chocolate in the insert of a double boiler. Bring water to a simmer in the bottom of the double boiler and reduce the heat until it's as low as it will go. (You can substitute a heat-proof bowl and any tall saucepan for the double boiler.) Put the insert into the double boiler, making sure the bottom of the insert does not touch the water. Let stand, stirring occasionally, until the chocolate is smooth and melted. Be careful not to get any water into the chocolate, as even a drop of water will make it seize and tighten. And watch out for overheating (chocolate is considered burned if heated above 130°F/54°C), or it will thicken and clump. In both cases, the chocolate will have to be discarded.

You can also melt chocolate in a microwave. Put the chocolate in a heat-proof, microwave-safe bowl. Microwave at medium (50 percent) power for 20-second intervals, stirring the chocolate after each interval, until it is smooth and melted. The chocolate may not look melted until after it is stirred. It is easy to overheat chocolate in the microwave, so take care.

SCRAPING

When mixing cake batter, we have a mantra: Scrape, scrape, scrape! A few times during mixing, stop the mixer and scrape the batter clinging to the sides and bottom of the bowl with a large rubber spatula. If you ignore this step, you will have a lumpy batter. Stand mixers are especially guilty of leaving unmixed batter at the bowl's bottom, although the BeaterBlade attachment does help.

SIFTING

Some baking books don't advise readers to sift the dry ingredients, and assume that it's enough to just stir or whisk everything together in a bowl. This is a mistake. Sifting aerates the flour so it blends well with other ingredients in the batter, and sifting also combines dry ingredients for even distribution. Perhaps most important, it breaks up lumps of baking soda and similar ingredients with a tendency to clump. If you have ever come across a lump of baking soda in a muffin, you know how it can ruin your morning. So please, don't skip the sifting.

We use a medium-mesh wire sieve for sifting because it is larger and quicker than a canister-style sifter. Don't use a fine-mesh sieve, as the weave is too tight to allow the dry ingredients to pass through. You can sift the ingredients into a bowl, and then transfer them to the batter with a large spatula or serving spoon. It is also useful to sift onto a large piece of parchment or wax paper, which can be lifted like a sling to let the ingredients slide into the mixing bowl.

TIMING

Just as you shouldn't guess at the size of pans or the length of croissant dough, don't depend on your inner sense of time when a cake is in the oven. Use a timer! That being said, remember that a timer is a tool, but your senses are the best indicators for telling when baked goods are done. Your nose will let you know that the sugars have caramelized and set, and you will smell a rich, toasted aroma. Use your fingertips to lightly press the top of a cake—if it springs back, it is finished. Sometimes, sight alone (a golden brown color) can show you whether the pastry is finished. Also, a cake layer will be shrinking away from the sides of the pan slightly when fully baked. Even our sense of hearing comes into play—rap your knuckles on the underside of a crusty loaf to hear the telltale hollow sound, a doneness indicator.

TOASTING NUTS

To toast most nuts, spread them out on a rimmed baking sheet and bake in a preheated 350°F/180°C/gas 4 oven, stirring occasionally, until they smell fragrant and have turned a slightly darker shade of brown, about 10 minutes.

To toast hazelnuts, bake until the skins are cracked and the flesh underneath is golden brown. Wrap the warm hazelnuts in a kitchen towel and let cool for 5 minutes. Using the towel, rub off the hazelnut skins. Don't worry if some of the skins stay attached.

WHIPPING EGG WHITES

Beaten egg whites have many uses in the baker's kitchen. They leaven batters, and are sweetened to make delicate meringues and to form the base for buttercream frosting. There are two things to consider when using egg whites: cleanliness and temperature.

Egg whites are protein and will not whip if the bowl contains the slightest bit of fat to inhibit their structure. (We have ruined a batch of whipped whites by accidentally flicking in a drop of cake batter.) Plastic bowls will retain a thin film of fat, so only use stainless-steel, glass, or ceramic bowls for whipping whites.

The whites will expand to their greatest capacity if they are around 60°F/16°C, or cool room temperature. To quickly bring refrigerated egg whites to the correct temperature, separate the whole eggs while they are still cold. (The yolk will be firmer and less likely to break during separating.) Put the whites in a very clean, heat-proof bowl. Put the bowl in a larger bowl of hot water and let stand, stirring the egg whites occasionally, just until they lose their chill, 3 to 5 minutes.

If you are whipping more than five whites, you can use a stand mixer fitted with the whisk attachment set on high speed. Less than five whites won't reach the bottom of the whisk, and a hand mixer or wire balloon whisk (with thin wires and a bulbous shape to beat the most air into the whites) is a better choice.

Egg whites are usually beaten to form either soft or stiff peaks. For soft peaks, whip the whites until the whisk or beaters leave a visible trail in the whites. Stop the mixer and lift the whisk or beaters; the whites in the bowl should form a peak with a drooping tip. This is the stage used in most batters. Be careful not to beat the whites to the point where they become dry-looking and clumpy.

Stiffly beaten egg whites usually include sugar to help stabilize the mixture. For stiff peaks, beat the whites until the mixture is thick and shiny. When the whisk or beaters are lifted, the tip of the peak will stand straight up without drooping.

WHEN IN DOUBT, MEASURE

A ruler and a yardstick may not seem like common kitchen tools, but relying on the size marked on the pan can be dicey because some manufacturers give the dimensions of the top of the pan and others measure the bottom, which can make for significant differences, especially when a pan has sloping sides. So take out the ruler and measure your pans.

A ruler is also handy to determine the thickness of a pie dough or how large to roll out a round of pastry to fit a tart pan. A yardstick will be needed to measure the doughs for the baked goods in the Yeasted Sweets chapter in order to cut them into precise shapes for even baking—a ruler would be too small.

BREADS

Our artisan breads established the reputation of the Model Bakery, as we were offering these crusty, tangy loaves before anyone else in the Valley. There was no more driving ninety minutes into San Francisco to get "real" bread, although the options there were few and far between, too. Bread making has changed a lot since those early years, and our bakers often utilize new techniques—for example, they will pull and fold wet dough by hand over a longer period of time to build flavor and texture instead of using the familiar method of kneading drier dough in a machine. However, there are still some doughs (usually for sandwich breads with a tight crumb) that are best made by kneading. We want to simplify the process of making bread as much as possible for you. There can be a lot of steps to making bread, but very little actual physical labor. Most of the time is spent waiting.

THE MODEL BAKERY'S
ENGLISH MUFFINS

MAKES 12 ENGLISH MUFFINS

Even though the bakery's doors had been open for over eighty years, these muffins put us on the national radar when they were featured on the Food Network's *The Best Thing I Ever Ate*. We used to make these the old-fashioned way, shaped in ring molds (actually, we made ours in old tuna cans, which you cannot do any more because the sizes have changed). When we realized we could shape them by hand, it changed our lives—literally—as everyone for miles around wanted to try this "new" free-form version. Our English muffins are quite large when compared to the supermarket variety, which makes them wonderful sandwich rolls as well as breakfast treats. A couple of notes: You will need a heavy skillet or griddle (preferably cast-iron) to make these. And be sure to make the biga at least 12 hours before making the dough. Since you will probably be toasting the muffins, they don't have to be fresh from the griddle; so make them a day or two ahead (or freeze them) if you wish.

BIGA

½ cup/75 g bread flour

¼ cup/60 ml water

¼ tsp instant (also called quick-rising or bread machine) yeast

DOUGH

1⅓ cups/315 ml water

¾ tsp instant (also called quick-rising or bread machine) yeast

1 Tbsp plus 1 tsp extra-virgin olive oil

1½ tsp fine sea salt

3½ cups/510 g unbleached all-purpose flour, as needed

¼ cup/35g yellow cornmeal, preferably stone-ground

6 Tbsp/90 ml melted Clarified Butter (page 37), as needed

1. **TO MAKE THE BIGA:** At least 1 day before cooking the muffins, combine the flour, water, and yeast in a small bowl to make a sticky dough. Cover tightly with plastic wrap and refrigerate for at least 12 hours or up to 24 hours. The biga will rise slightly.

2. **TO MAKE THE DOUGH:** Combine the biga, water, yeast, olive oil, and salt in the bowl of a stand mixer. Affix the bowl to the mixer and fit with the paddle attachment. Mix on low speed until the mixture looks creamy, about 1 minute. Mix in 3 cups/435 g of the flour to make a soft, sticky dough. Turn off the mixer, cover the bowl with plastic wrap, and let stand for 20 minutes. (To make by hand, combine the water, biga, yeast, oil, and salt in a large bowl and break up the biga with a wooden spoon. Stir until the biga dissolves. Mix in enough flour to make a cohesive but tacky dough. Cover and let stand for 20 minutes.)

3. Mix in enough of the remaining flour to make a soft dough that barely cleans the mixer bowl. Replace the paddle with the dough hook. Knead on medium-low speed (if the dough climbs up the hook, just pull it down) until the dough is smooth and elastic, about 8 minutes. Turn out the dough onto a lightly floured work surface to check its texture. It should feel tacky but not stick to the work surface. (To make by hand, knead on a floured work surface, adding more flour as necessary, until the dough is smooth and feels tacky, about 10 minutes.)

CONTINUED

4. Shape the dough into a ball. Oil a medium bowl. Put the dough in the bowl and turn to coat with oil, leaving the dough smooth-side up. Cover with plastic wrap. Let stand in a warm place until almost doubled in volume, about 2 hours. (The dough can also be refrigerated for 8 to 12 hours. Let stand at room temperature for 1 hour before proceeding to the next step.)

5. Using a bowl scraper, scrape the dough out of the bowl onto a lightly floured work surface. Cut into twelve equal pieces. Shape each into a 4-in/10-cm round. Sprinkle an even layer of cornmeal over a half-sheet pan. Place the rounds on the cornmeal about 1 in/2.5 cm apart. Turn the rounds to coat both sides with cornmeal. Loosely cover the pan with plastic wrap. Let stand in a warm place until the rounds have increased in volume by half and a finger pressed into a round leaves an impression for a few seconds before filling up, about 1 hour.

6. Melt 2 Tbsp of the clarified butter in a large, heavy skillet (preferably cast-iron) over medium heat until melted and hot, but not smoking. In batches, add the dough rounds to the skillet. Cook, adjusting the heat as needed so the muffins brown without scorching, adding more clarified butter as needed. The undersides should be nicely browned, about 6 minutes. Turn and cook until the other sides are browned and the muffins are puffed, about 6 minutes more. Transfer to a paper towel–lined half-sheet pan and let cool. (It will be tempting to eat these hot off the griddle, but let them stand for at least 20 minutes to complete the cooking with carry-over heat.) Repeat with the remaining muffins, wiping the cornmeal out of the skillet with paper towels and adding more clarified butter as needed.

7. Split each muffin in half horizontally with a serrated knife. Toast in a broiler or toaster oven (they may be too thick for a standard toaster) until lightly browned. Serve hot. (The muffins can be stored in an airtight container at room temperature for up to 2 days.)

CLARIFIED BUTTER

MAKES ABOUT ¾ CUP/180 ML

Our decadent English muffins are cooked in butter, a great cooking medium with one major drawback—the milk solids in butter burn easily. Clarifying the butter is an easy process that removes the milk solids. Leftover clarified butter can be used like oil for sautéing food. It keeps for a few weeks in a refrigerated covered container.

---

1 lb/455 g unsalted butter, cut up

1. Melt the butter in a small saucepan over medium heat until completely melted and boiling. Cook until the butter stops sputtering, about 1 minute. Remove from the heat and let stand for 5 minutes. Skim the foam from the surface of the butter.

2. Line a wire sieve with dampened, wrung-out cheesecloth and place over a medium bowl. Carefully pour the clear, yellow melted butter through the sieve, leaving the milky residue behind in the saucepan. (Discard the residue.) Pour into a small container and cover. Refrigerate until ready to use.

DINNER ROLLS

MAKES 18 ROLLS

At Thanksgiving it seems as if every family in the Valley places an order for our old-fashioned dinner rolls; we sell more than a thousand in one day. We've gotten to the point where we just don't have the space in our ovens for more rolls and we have to turn down orders, which any business owner hates to do. These are excellent shaped into hamburger buns, so see the variations when you want to ratchet up the quality of your backyard cookout with homemade buns.

Butter, at room temperature, for the pans

1 recipe Pain de Mie dough, made through step 4 (see page 46)

Flour for sprinkling

1. Lightly butter two 9-in/23-cm round cake pans that have 1½-in/4-cm sides. Turn the dough out onto an unfloured work surface and deflate it with your fingertips. Cut the dough into eighteen equal pieces. Place them on the work surface and cover loosely with plastic wrap.

2. Place a piece of dough in front of you on the work surface. Cup your dominant hand over the dough, letting your palm touch the top of the dough. Quickly move your hand in a tight circle over the dough to shape it into a smooth ball. (It takes a little practice, but once you get it down, you may even be able to roll two balls at once, one under each hand.) Arrange nine balls in each pan, allowing room for expansion between the balls. Cover each pan loosely with plastic wrap. Let stand in a warm place until almost doubled in volume, about 45 minutes.

3. Position a rack in the center of the oven and preheat to 350°F/180°C/gas 4.

4. Sprinkle the rolls with flour. Bake until the rolls are golden brown, about 25 minutes. Let cool in the pans for 5 minutes. The rolls can be cooled, transferred to freezer storage bags, and frozen for up to 1 month. Thaw the frozen rolls for 1 hour. Wrap in aluminum foil and bake in a preheated 350°F/180°C/gas 4 oven until warm, about 15 minutes.

HAMBURGER BUNS: Cut the dough into eight equal pieces. Shape each piece into a ball. Press hard on the ball to flatten into a disk about 4 in/10 cm in diameter. Place the disks about 2 in/5 cm apart on a parchment paper–lined baking sheet. Cover loosely with plastic wrap and let rise until almost doubled, about 45 minutes. Glaze, sprinkle with seeds, and bake as directed until golden brown.

SEEDED ROLLS: Omit the flour topping. Beat together 1 large egg yolk and 2 tbsp heavy cream in a small bowl. Brush the tops of the rolls lightly with the egg mixture. Sprinkle each pan of rolls with 2 tsp sesame or poppy seeds. Bake as directed.

CIABATTA

MAKES 1 LOAF

In the San Francisco Bay Area, we have a long-standing love for crusty bread, but it took some time for the rest of the country to catch up. Ciabatta's wide, elongated shape (*ciabatta* means "slipper" in Italian) ensures lots of crackly crust, and it is now sold in just about every supermarket. The dough is especially wet and sticky, so you will need a stand mixer to make it. We are very proud of our version, which we supply to some of the best Italian restaurants in the area. We make a customized recipe for Bottega Ristorante in Yountville, using Michael Chiarello's imported gray sea salt. It is the perfect bread for dipping in olive oil.

BIGA

¾ cup plus 1 Tbsp/120 g bread flour

½ cup/120 ml water

⅛ tsp instant (also called quick-rising or bread machine) yeast

DOUGH

¾ cup/180 ml water

1¼ tsp fine sea salt

½ tsp instant (also called quick-rising or bread machine) yeast

2 cups/290 g bread flour

Semolina for the parchment paper

1. **TO MAKE THE BIGA:** Combine the flour, water, and yeast in a small bowl to make a thick, lumpy batter. Cover with plastic wrap and let stand in a warm place until the surface shows bubbles, about 2 hours.

2. **TO MAKE THE DOUGH:** Combine the biga, water, salt, and yeast in the bowl of a stand mixer. Affix the bowl to the mixer and fit with the paddle attachment. Mix on low speed until the mixture looks creamy. Gradually add the flour and mix just until the dough is cohesive, but very sticky. Turn off the mixer, cover the bowl with a kitchen towel, and let stand for 20 minutes.

3. Replace the paddle with the dough hook. Knead on medium-low speed (if the dough climbs up the hook, just pull it down) until the dough is smooth and tacky, with a thick, batter-like texture, about 5 minutes.

4. Cover the bowl of dough with plastic wrap. Let stand in a warm place until almost doubled in volume, about 1½ hours.

5. Pull one-quarter of the dough up and over onto the top of the dough. Repeat with the other three-quarters of the dough. Cover again and let stand until almost doubled, about 45 minutes.

6. Using a bowl scraper, turn out the dough onto a well-floured work surface. (Do not punch the dough down; you want to retain as many of the air pockets as possible.) Using floured hands, tuck the sides of the sticky dough under to shape into a rectangle about 12 in/30.5 cm long and 6 in/15 cm wide. Place a sheet of parchment paper on a baker's peel or rimless baking sheet and sprinkle generously with semolina. Lift and transfer the loaf, smooth-side

up, to the parchment paper and reshape the loaf as needed. Flour the top of the dough well (to keep the rack from sticking to the dough) and cover loosely with plastic wrap. Let stand in a warm place until the dough looks inflated but not doubled, about 45 minutes.

7. Position two racks on the lowest two rungs of the oven. Put a baking stone on the top rack and an empty broiler pan on the lower one. Preheat the oven to 450°F/230°C/gas 8. When the oven is preheated, using a kettle, pour about 2 cups/480 ml hot water into the hot broiler pan. Close the oven door and let it heat for 5 minutes more to fill the oven with steam (it may not be visible).

8. Slide the loaf with the parchment paper onto the baking stone in the oven. Bake for 20 minutes. Reduce the oven temperature to 400°F/200°C/gas 6. Bake until the bread is deep golden brown and sounds hollow when tapped on the bottom, about 20 minutes more. Using the baker's peel, transfer the ciabatta to a wire cooling rack and let cool for at least 20 minutes before slicing. The ciabatta can be wrapped in aluminum foil and stored at room temperature for up to 1 day.

FOCACCIA

MAKES 8 TO 12 PIECES

Like ciabatta, focaccia is a bread that hardly anyone in the United States knew about a couple of decades ago. It should be light and airy, and thick enough to slice horizontally to make into sandwiches. This is made without a pre-ferment, so you can start in the morning and bake a batch for lunch.

5½ cups/800 g unbleached all-purpose flour, as needed

2⅓ cups plus 2 Tbsp/585 ml water

2 Tbsp extra-virgin olive oil, plus more for the bowl and brushing

1 Tbsp instant (also called quick-rising or bread machine) yeast

2½ tsp fine sea salt

1½ tsp finely chopped fresh rosemary

1½ tsp finely chopped fresh flat-leaf parsley

Kosher salt for sprinkling

1. Combine 4 cups/580 g of the flour with the water, olive oil, yeast, and sea salt in the bowl of a stand mixer. Affix the bowl to the mixer and fit with the paddle attachment. Mix on low speed just until the dough is cohesive. Turn off the mixer, cover the bowl with plastic wrap, and let stand for 10 minutes. (To make by hand, combine the water, yeast, oil, and sea salt in a large bowl. Mix in enough of the flour to make a cohesive, tacky dough. Cover and let stand for 20 minutes.)

2. Replace the paddle with the dough hook. Knead on medium-low speed, adding enough of the remaining flour as necessary to make a soft dough that doesn't stick to the bowl. Continue kneading until the dough is smooth and slightly tacky, about 6 minutes, scraping the dough down off the hook as necessary. Mix in the rosemary and parsley. Turn out the dough onto a floured work surface. (To make by hand, knead on a floured work surface, adding more flour as necessary to make a smooth and elastic but slightly tacky dough, about 10 minutes. Flatten the dough into a rectangle and sprinkle with the rosemary and parsley. Roll up the dough and knead briefly to distribute the herbs.)

3. Shape the dough into a ball. Lightly oil a medium bowl. Put the dough in the bowl and turn to coat with oil, leaving the dough smooth-side up. Cover tightly with plastic wrap. Let stand in a warm place until doubled in volume, about 1½ hours.

4. Lightly oil a half-sheet pan. Turn the dough out onto the pan. Using oiled hands, stretch and pat the dough to fill the pan. If the dough is too elastic from the activated gluten and retracts (and it probably will), cover the dough with a kitchen towel and let stand for about 10 minutes to relax the gluten. Be sure the dough fills the corners of the pan. Cover with a kitchen towel and let stand until the dough rises to the top of the pan, about 1 hour.

5. Position a rack in the center of the oven and preheat to 400°F/200°C/gas 6. Dimple the top of the dough with your fingertips. Lightly brush the dough with olive oil and sprinkle with kosher salt.

6. Bake until the focaccia is golden brown, about 30 minutes. Let cool in the pan for at least 5 minutes. Cut into large rectangles and serve. Focaccia is best the day of baking.

STRUAN

MAKES 1 LOAF

Struan was popularized by master baker Peter Reinhardt, who had a bakery in Santa Rosa, California, not too far from us. (Now he is passing on his deep knowledge of bread making to students at Johnson & Wales University in Charlotte, North Carolina.) This multigrain bread, which Peter says originated in Scotland, is as delicious as it is versatile. Our version is a tad less sweet than Peter's. We use it for our all-purpose bread—perfect for sandwiches and excellent as toast. Begin the night before you bake by soaking the grains and making a biga (a simple starter). Struan could become your go-to bread.

SOAKER

¼ cup/60 ml water

3 Tbsp coarse cornmeal (polenta)

3 Tbsp old-fashioned (rolled) oats or wheat or rye flakes

2 Tbsp wheat or oat bran

BIGA

½ cup/75 g bread flour

¼ tsp instant (also called quick-rising or bread machine) yeast

½ cup/120 ml water

DOUGH

½ cup/120 ml buttermilk

¼ cup/60 ml water

1½ Tbsp honey

2¾ tsp instant (also called quick-rising or bread machine) yeast

2½ cups/365 g bread flour, as needed

3 Tbsp cooked brown rice (see Note)

1½ tsp fine sea salt

Vegetable oil for the bowl and pan

2 Tbsp poppy seeds

1. **TO MAKE THE SOAKER:** Combine the water, cornmeal, oats, and bran in a small bowl. The water will barely moisten the grains. Cover and let stand at room temperature for 12 to 16 hours.

2. **TO MAKE THE BIGA:** Combine the flour, yeast, and water in a small bowl until well blended. Cover with plastic wrap and let stand at room temperature for 12 to 16 hours. The mixture will be bubbly.

3. **TO MAKE THE DOUGH:** Combine the soaker, biga, buttermilk, water, honey, and yeast in the bowl of a stand mixer. Add 2¼ cups/325 g of the flour and the rice and salt. Affix the bowl to the mixer and fit with the paddle attachment. Mix on low speed just until the dough is cohesive. Turn off the mixer, cover the bowl with a kitchen towel, and let stand for 20 minutes. (To make by hand, combine the soaker, biga, buttermilk, water, honey, yeast, and rice in a large bowl. Stir in enough of the flour to make a soft dough. Cover and let stand.)

4. Replace the paddle with the dough hook. Knead on medium-low speed, adding enough of the remaining flour to make a soft, smooth, and tacky dough that cleans the bowl, about 6 minutes. Turn out the dough onto a lightly floured work surface. (To make by hand, knead on a floured work surface, adding more flour as necessary, for about 10 minutes.)

5. Shape the dough into a ball. Lightly oil a medium bowl. Put the dough in the bowl and turn to coat with oil, leaving the dough smooth-side up. Cover tightly with plastic wrap. Let stand at room temperature until doubled in volume, about 90 minutes.

6. Lightly oil a 9-by-5-by-3-in/23-by-12-by-7.5-cm loaf pan. Turn out the dough (it will be quite soft) onto an unfloured work surface. Pat into a thick rectangle 9 in/23 cm long. Roll up and pinch the seam closed. Turn the loaf seam-side down and spray all over with water. Sprinkle the top and sides with poppy seeds. Fit into the

CONTINUED

STRUAN

CONTINUED

prepared pan, seam-side down, and pat the dough to fill the pan evenly, especially into the corners. Cover loosely with plastic wrap and let stand at room temperature just until the dough begins to dome over the top of the pan, about 90 minutes.

7. Position a rack in the center of the oven and put a baking stone on the rack. Preheat the oven to 350°F/180°C/gas 4.

8. Bake, rotating the pan 180 degrees after 20 minutes, until the loaf is golden brown and the bottom sounds hollow when rapped with your knuckles (remove the loaf from the pan to check), about 45 minutes. Let cool in the pan for 5 minutes. Remove from the pan and let cool on a wire cooling rack for at least 30 minutes before slicing. The bread can be wrapped in aluminum foil and stored at room temperature for up to 1 day.

NOTE: *Rather than make just 3 Tbsp of cooked brown rice for this bread, make enough to serve for a meal. Reserve 3 Tbsp until ready to use. It will keep in an airtight container in the refrigerator for up to 3 days and in the freezer for up to 3 months. Thaw before using.*

PAIN DE MIE

MAKES 1 LOAF

For a crusty loaf with what bakers call an open crumb, all you need is flour, water, yeast, and salt. Take the same ingredients and enrich them with eggs, butter, milk, and a little sugar, and you'll get a tender loaf with a cakelike crumb, perfect for slicing. The French go so far as to call this kind of loaf *pain de mie*, which literally means "crumb loaf." (However, our French baker, Pascal, christened it "inside bread," because it is a loaf that is all about the inside of the bread.) As the bread cools, you can play a game with yourself: How long can you wait before you cut into it and spread a warm slice with butter?

POOLISH

⅓ cup/50 g bread flour

⅓ cup/75 ml water

⅛ tsp instant (also called quick-rising or bread machine) yeast

DOUGH

⅓ cup/75 ml whole milk

⅓ cup/75 ml water

2 large eggs

1 Tbsp plus 1 tsp sugar

2⅛ tsp instant (also called quick-rising or bread machine) yeast

1½ tsp fine sea salt

3½ cups/510 g bread flour, as needed

3 Tbsp unsalted butter, at room temperature

1. **TO MAKE THE POOLISH:** Combine the flour, water, and yeast in a small bowl to make a thick, lumpy batter. Cover with plastic wrap and let stand in a warm place until the top looks foamy, about 1½ hours.

2. **TO MAKE THE DOUGH:** Scrape the poolish into the bowl of a stand mixer and add the milk, water, eggs, sugar, yeast, and salt. Affix the bowl to the mixer and fit with the paddle attachment. Mix on low speed until the mixture looks creamy. Gradually add 3 cups/435 g of the flour and mix just until the dough is cohesive. Turn off the mixer, cover the bowl with a kitchen towel, and let stand for 10 minutes. (To make by hand, mix the poolish, milk, water, eggs, sugar, yeast, and salt together in a large bowl. Mix in enough of the flour to make a cohesive, tacky dough. Cover and let stand.)

3. Replace the paddle with the dough hook. With the machine on medium-low speed, add the butter, 1 Tbsp at a time, letting the dough absorb each addition before adding more. Knead on medium-low speed, adding more flour as necessary, to make a soft, supple, and slightly tacky dough, about 8 minutes. Turn out the dough onto a lightly floured work surface. (To make by hand, cut the butter into small cubes and sprinkle one-third of it over the dough. Working in the bowl, using floured hands, pull up about one-quarter of the dough, stretching it about 10 in/25 cm, and fold over the top of the dough. Repeat, one-quarter at a time. Using your knuckles, knead the dough in the bowl until the butter is absorbed. Repeat two more times with the remaining butter. Turn the dough out onto a floured

work surface. Knead, adding more flour as necessary, until the dough is smooth, soft, and slightly tacky, about 10 minutes.)

4. Lightly butter a large bowl. Shape the dough into a ball, put in bowl, and turn to coat with butter, leaving the dough smooth-side up. Cover with plastic wrap. Let stand in a warm place until doubled in volume, about 1½ hours.

5. Lightly butter a 9-by-5-by-3-in/23-by-12-by-7.5-cm loaf pan. Turn out the dough onto the work surface. Press and shape into a rectangle 9 in/23 cm long. Fold the top and bottom edges over to meet in the middle of the rectangle and pinch the seam closed. Fit into the pan, seam-side down, pressing the dough gently so it fills the corners. Cover loosely with plastic wrap and let stand in a warm place until the dough just begins to peek over the top of the pan, about 45 minutes.

6. Position a rack in the center of the oven and preheat to 350°F/180°C/gas 4.

7. Bake until the loaf is golden brown and sounds hollow when rapped with your knuckles (remove the loaf from the pan to check), about 45 minutes. Let cool in the pan for 10 minutes. Remove from the pan and let cool on a wire cooling rack for at least 20 minutes before slicing. The bread can be wrapped in aluminum foil and stored at room temperature for up to 1 day.

PAIN AU LEVAIN

MAKES 2 LOAVES

Our flavorful, crusty, chewy pain au levain and its variations are served at many events at various Napa wineries throughout the year. When Karen first learned to bake, there was only one way to make artisan bread at home—knead the starter-leavened dough by hand or machine and bake it, uncovered, on a baking stone. Thanks to the detailed instruction in cookbooks by Chad Robertson, Jim Lahey, Karen's old friend Peter Reinhart, and others, there have been many advances in how home bakers make bread, resulting in baked goods that truly seem like they came from the best bakeries in the world. At the Model Bakery, our lead baker, Eli Colvin, developed a modern recipe for the home baker that replicates the levain bread (and its three variations) that we deliver throughout the Valley. Note that you will need two 8-in/20-cm round bannetons (see page 61) or colanders.

LEVAIN

½ cup/120 ml water

1 Tbsp Wild Yeast Grape Starter (page 56)

⅓ cup/50 g bread flour

⅓ cup/50 g whole-wheat flour

DOUGH

3⅓ cups/795 ml water

5¾ cups plus 2 Tbsp/850 g bread flour, plus more as needed

⅔ cup/95 g whole-wheat flour

1½ Tbsp fine sea salt

Semolina for the baker's peel

1. **TO MAKE THE LEVAIN:** The night before baking, mix the water and starter together in a small bowl. Add the bread flour and the whole-wheat flour and stir to make a thick batter. Cover tightly with plastic wrap and refrigerate for 8 to 12 hours.

2. **TO MAKE THE DOUGH:** The next morning, combine the water and levain in the bowl of a stand mixer. Mix with the paddle attachment on low speed until combined. Gradually add the flours to make a sticky dough. Do not remove the paddle. Cover the bowl with plastic wrap and let stand for 20 minutes. (To make by hand, stir the water and levain together in a large bowl. Gradually stir in the flours to make a wet, sticky dough. Cover and let stand for 20 minutes.)

3. With the mixer on low speed, mix the salt into the dough. Remove the paddle.

(Or, to make by hand, sprinkle the salt over the dough. Using wet hands, squeeze the dough well to mix in the salt.) Cover the bowl with plastic wrap and let stand for 20 minutes.

4. As the flour absorbs the liquid, the dough will look a bit firmer and less wet. Using wet hands, pull up about one-quarter of the dough, stretching it about 10 in/25 cm, and fold over the top of the dough. Repeat, one-quarter at a time. Cover with plastic wrap and let stand for 20 minutes.

5. The dough will continue to firm up. (If you are making one of the variations, add the additional ingredients at this point.) Repeat the pulling and folding process, cover with plastic wrap, and let stand for 20 minutes.

CONTINUED

6. The dough will be somewhat firmer and will have risen slightly, but not doubled. Repeat the pulling and folding process a third time.

7. Using a bowl scraper to release the dough from the bowl, turn out the dough onto a well-floured work surface. The dough will be very tacky, but that is what you want. The flour on the work surface will keep the dough from sticking. Do not punch the dough down; you want to retain as many of the air pockets as possible. Cut the dough in half. Place one portion of dough in front of you on a lightly floured work surface. Cupping your hands slightly, place them on either side of the dough. Tuck the sides of the dough underneath the mass, gently stretching the surface of the dough to make it taut. Repeat with the remaining dough.

8. Generously dust the insides of two 8-in/20-cm round bannetons with flour. Or line each of two 8-in/20-cm colanders or bowls with linen or cotton (but not terry cloth) towels and coat with flour. Be sure the banneton or cloth is well floured so the dough won't stick. Turn each ball upside down and place, smooth-side down, in a banneton. Pinch the loose ends of the loaf together. Sprinkle more flour over each. Loosely cover each banneton with plastic wrap. Let stand in a warm place until the dough looks slightly inflated but not doubled (when poked with a fingertip, the hole left will fill in slowly), about 2 hours.

9. Position a rack in the lower third in the oven and place a baking stone on the rack. Put a metal pot (with heat-proof handles) with about a 6-qt/5.7-L capacity, and at least 9 in/23 cm in diameter, upside down on the stone. Preheat the oven, with the stone and pot, to 500°F/260°C/gas 10.

10. Sprinkle a baker's peel with semolina. Carefully turn out one loaf onto the peel. The dough will be soft and will spread slightly on the peel. Using a serrated knife, quickly cut a shallow 4-in/10-cm square in the top of the ball. If the kitchen is very warm, refrigerate the remaining loaf while baking the first.

11. The next set of steps will happen quickly; read over the directions a couple of times so you understand the process and can move with confidence. Put on oven mitts or equip yourself with thick pot holders. Open the oven, grab the hot pot by its sides and put the pot, still upside down, on top of the stove. Slide the rack with the stone out of the oven slightly. Slip the loaf off the peel onto the stone. Replace the pot, upside down, over the loaf so that the pot doesn't touch the dough. Slide the rack back into the oven and close the oven door. Bake for 20 minutes.

12. Using the pot holders, remove the pot, leaving the bread in place. Reduce the oven temperature to 450°F/230°C/gas 8. Continue baking until the bread is deep golden brown and sounds hollow when tapped on the bottom, about 20 minutes more. If you have any concerns about whether the bread is done, you can take its temperature through the bottom crust with an instant-read thermometer; it should read at least 190°F/88°C.

13. Using the baker's peel, transfer the bread to a wire cooling rack. Repeat with the remaining dough. Let cool for at least 20 minutes before slicing. The bread can be wrapped in aluminum foil and stored at room temperature for up to 1 day.

TOASTED WALNUT AND SAGE BREAD: Add 2 cups/230 g coarsely chopped toasted walnuts (see page 30) and 2 Tbsp chopped fresh sage to the dough in step 5 and fold as directed.

AUTUMN PAIN AU LEVAIN: Add 1 cup/170 g dried cranberries and 1 cup/115 g coarsely chopped toasted walnuts (see page 30) to the dough in step 5 and fold as directed.

COUNTRY OLIVE PAIN AU LEVAIN WITH ROSEMARY: Add 1 cup/155 g pitted and coarsely chopped black and green olives (we use an herbed Provençal mix from France) and 2 Tbsp chopped fresh rosemary in step 5 and fold as directed.

WHOLE-WHEAT HARVEST BREAD

MAKES 1 LOAF

Here is a whole-wheat bread with everything going for it. It gets a little tang from the starter, a bit of sweetness (but not too much) from the honey, and a tender crumb from the vegetable oil. Where many whole-wheat breads are, in reality, mostly white flour with some whole wheat tossed in as an afterthought, this loaf reverses the proportions. It is another bread that you will cherish when it comes time to make your lunchtime sandwich. Take care not to add too much flour during kneading. The dough should be tacky (on the edge of sticky); it will firm up during fermentation.

1⅔ cups/405 ml water

½ cup/160 g Wild Yeast Grape Starter (page 56)

1½ Tbsp honey

2½ tsp fine sea salt

2 tsp vegetable oil, plus more for the bowl

1¼ tsp instant (also called quick-rising or bread machine) yeast

3 cups/435 g whole-wheat flour

1 cup/145 g bread flour, plus more as needed

1 large egg yolk

1 Tbsp heavy cream or milk

2 tsp wheat bran

1. Combine the water, starter, honey, salt, vegetable oil, and yeast in the bowl of a stand mixer. Affix the bowl to the mixer and fit with the paddle attachment. Mix on low speed until the mixture looks creamy. Gradually add the whole-wheat flour and ½ cup/75 g of the bread flour to make a cohesive but sticky dough. Turn off the mixer, cover the bowl with a kitchen towel, and let stand for 20 minutes. (To make by hand, combine the water, starter, honey, salt, oil, and yeast in a large bowl. Stir in the whole-wheat flour and enough of the bread flour to make a cohesive but sticky dough. Cover and let stand.)

2. Replace the paddle with the dough hook. Knead on medium speed, adding enough of the remaining bread flour to make a somewhat tacky dough that cleans the bowl, about 8 minutes. Turn out the dough onto a floured work surface. (To make by hand, knead on a floured work surface, using a bench scraper to help lift the dough and adding more flour as necessary to form a soft, tacky dough that barely sticks to the work surface, about 10 minutes.)

3. Shape the dough into a ball. Lightly oil a medium bowl. Put the dough in the bowl and turn to coat with oil, leaving the dough smooth-side up. Cover the bowl with plastic wrap. Let stand in a warm place until doubled in volume, 1½ to 2 hours.

4. Lightly oil a 9-by-5-by-3-in/23-by-12-by-7.5-cm loaf pan. Using a bowl scraper, scrape the dough out of the bowl onto a lightly floured work surface. Shape the dough into a 9-in/23-cm square. Starting from the bottom, roll up the dough and pinch the seams closed. Transfer to the pan, long-seam-side down. Lightly press the dough into the pan, being sure it fills the corners. Cover loosely with plastic wrap and let stand in a warm place until the dough has doubled and risen to the top of the pan, about 1 hour.

5. Position a rack in the center of the oven and put a baking stone on the rack. Preheat the oven to 400°F/200°C/gas 6.

6. Beat the egg yolk and cream together in a small bowl. Lightly brush the top of the loaf with the glaze. Sprinkle with the bran.

7. Bake for 15 minutes. Reduce the heat to 350°F/180°C/gas 4 and bake until the bottom of the loaf sounds hollow when rapped with your knuckles (remove the loaf from the pan to check), about 35 minutes more. Let cool in the pan for 10 minutes. Remove from the pan. Transfer to a wire cooling rack and let cool for at least 20 minutes before slicing. The bread can be wrapped in aluminum foil and stored at room temperature for up to 1 day.

AMBER ALE BREAD

MAKES 1 LARGE LOAF

Just north of St. Helena stands a gorgeous stone building that once housed Silverado Brewing Company. A few years ago, the owners, Michael Fradelizio and Ken Mee (a former student of Karen's when she was a high school teacher!), asked us to develop a recipe using their amber ale. One of our lead bakers, Eli Colvin, created this sturdy, flavorful loaf, which makes terrific sandwiches. Make a corned beef sandwich with it, and you may never go back to regular rye again. In this recipe, we set up a hot pan to create steam in the oven to encourage a crisp crust.

2 cups/480 ml amber ale (see Note)

1¼ tsp instant (also called quick-rising or bread machine) yeast

4¼ cups/615 g unbleached all-purpose flour, as needed

¾ cup/110 g whole-wheat flour

⅓ cup/50 g rye flour

2 tsp fine sea salt

Olive oil for the bowl and pans

Semolina for the baker's peel

1 large egg yolk

1 Tbsp heavy cream or milk

2 tsp wheat bran

1. Combine the ale and yeast in the bowl of a stand mixer. Add 2 cups/290 g of the all-purpose flour, the whole-wheat flour, rye flour, and salt. Affix the bowl to the mixer and fit with the paddle attachment. Mix on low speed, gradually adding enough of the remaining all-purpose flour to make a shaggy mass. Turn off the mixer, cover the bowl with plastic wrap, and let stand for 10 minutes. (To make by hand, combine the ale and yeast in a large bowl. Stir in the whole-wheat flour, rye flour, salt, and enough of the all-purpose flour to make a shaggy mass. Cover and let stand.)

2. Replace the paddle with the dough hook. Knead on medium-low speed, adding more all-purpose flour as necessary to make a smooth dough that cleans the sides of the bowl, about 6 minutes. Turn out the dough onto a floured work surface. (To make by hand, knead on a floured work surface, adding more flour as necessary to make a smooth, slightly tacky dough, about 10 minutes.)

3. Lightly oil a large bowl. Shape the dough into a ball, put in the bowl, and turn to coat with oil, leaving the dough smooth-side up. Cover with plastic wrap. Let stand in a warm place until doubled in volume, about 2 hours. (Or refrigerate for up to 16 hours. Let the dough stand at room temperature for 2 hours before proceeding.)

4. Turn out the dough onto a lightly floured work surface. Pat the dough into a thick rectangle about 12 in/30.5 cm long. Bring the long sides up to meet in the center and pinch the long seam closed. Turn the loaf over so the seam faces down. Tuck the sides of the loaf under to make a taut surface and taper the ends to make a torpedo-shaped loaf (*bâtard*) about 12 in/30.5 cm long and 4½ in/11 cm across at the widest point. Sprinkle a baker's peel generously with semolina. Transfer the loaf to the peel. Cover with a kitchen towel and let stand in a warm place until the dough looks inflated but not doubled, about 45 minutes.

5. Position two racks on the lowest two rungs of the oven. Put a baking stone on the top rack and an empty broiler pan on the lower one. Preheat the oven to 450°F/230°C/gas 8. When the oven is preheated, using a kettle, pour about 2 cups/480 ml hot water into the broiler pan. Close the oven door and let it heat for 5 minutes to fill the oven with steam (it may not be visible).

6. Beat the egg yolk and cream together in a small bowl. Starting about 2 in/5 cm from one end of the loaf, brush a strip of egg glaze about 1 in/2.5 cm wide across the width of the loaf. Repeat on the other side. Sprinkle each strip with about 1 tsp of the wheat bran. Using a serrated knife, cut a slash about ¼ in/6 mm deep along the edge of each bran–covered strip that is closest to the middle of the loaf.

7. Slip the loaf off the peel onto the baking stone. Bake for 20 minutes. Reduce the oven temperature to 425°F/220°C/gas 7. Continue baking until the top is golden brown and the bottom sounds hollow when rapped with your knuckles (remove the loaf from the pan to check) about 20 minutes more. Transfer to a wire cooling rack. Let cool for at least 20 minutes before slicing. The bread can be wrapped in aluminum foil and stored at room temperature for up to 1 day.

NOTE: *When measuring the ale, stir it well to dissipate the foamy head so you get an accurate measurement. If you have the time, open the bottle a couple of hours before measuring so the ale goes flat, which will make for foam–free measuring and won't affect the dough.*

WILD YEAST GRAPE STARTER

MAKES ABOUT 3 CUPS/960 G

We base many of our artisan breads on a fermented culture made from the local wine grapes. The first batch was created in the early years of the bakery. Many strains of wild yeast thrive on the fruit, so Karen knew that it wouldn't be difficult to "catch" the yeast. She simply crushed Gamay grapes in a big container, stirred in flour to make a batter, covered the mixture with cheesecloth to keep out fruit flies, and came back in a few days to a terrific goo that could be used to make bread rise. At home, it is easier to use freshly made grape juice. You can use any grapes, but we certainly recommend local organic fruit, if available, and if the grapes are a wine variety, so much the better. The amount of yeast and bacteria in your personal micro-climate (to be specific, your kitchen) and the ambient temperature affect the process, so plan on at least a week for fermentation and aging to allow for variables.

If a translucent brown or gray liquid forms on top of the starter at any time during the process, don't be alarmed. It is just the alcohol created during fermentation. Simply stir it in before using the starter. If the liquid is pink or if the starter smells unappetizingly funky, you have captured unwanted bacteria. Throw out the starter and start again.

DAY ONE

9 oz/255 g grapes on the stem (any variety), preferably organic wine grapes

½ cup/120 ml water, plus more as needed

¾ cup/110 g bread flour, plus more as needed

¼ cup/35 g whole-wheat flour

2 Tbsp rye flour

DAY TWO

½ cup/75 g bread flour

⅓ cup/75 ml water

DAY THREE

½ cup/75 g bread flour

⅓ cup/75 ml water

DAY FOUR

½ cup/75 g bread flour

⅓ cup/75 ml water

TO MAINTAIN THE STARTER

1 cup plus 2 Tbsp/165 g bread flour

¾ cup/180 ml water

DAY ONE: Remove the grapes from the stems and put the grapes in a bowl. Mash and crush with a potato masher or pestle to extract the juice. Strain through a wire sieve and discard the seeds and skins. Measure ¼ cup/60 ml and discard (or drink) the remaining juice.

Combine the grape juice, water, bread flour, whole-wheat flour, and rye flour in a 3-qt/2.8-L transparent bowl or container with a rubber spatula to make a sticky, wet dough (almost a batter). Scrape down the sides of the bowl. Cover the bowl loosely with plastic wrap to let in some air, and let stand at room temperature for 24 hours.

CONTINUED

DAY TWO: The mixture should show some small bubbles breaking on the surface and have a sharp aroma. (If not, let the mixture stand for another 24 hours.) Stir the bread flour and water into the mixture. Scrape down the sides of the bowl. Cover tightly this time to entrap the fermenting yeast and bacteria, and let stand for 24 hours.

DAY THREE: At this point, you should see more active bubbling and the mixture should smell like tart apples. Stir the bread flour and water into the mixture. Scrape down the sides of the bowl, cover tightly, and let stand for 24 hours.

DAY FOUR: The mixture should look like thick pancake batter, and if your container is clear, you will see a transparent network of bubbles through the side of the container. Stir in the bread flour and water. Mark the level of the starter on the outside of the bowl or container with a marker or a piece of masking tape so you can check how much the starter rises. Scrape down the sides of the bowl, cover tightly, and let stand until the starter doubles, deflates, and rises again, about 24 hours. (Let the starter stand for another 12 hours if the rising and deflating doesn't occur.)

DAY FIVE: The culture is almost fully developed and will smell appetizingly sour, with an aroma reminiscent of yogurt or cheese. Stir the starter to deflate it. Cover the bowl tightly and refrigerate for 2 days to age and strengthen the culture before using.

TO MAINTAIN THE STARTER: The starter must be refreshed once a week. Stir well to mix in the liquid that has formed on the surface. Discard (or use or give to a fellow baker) about half (around 1½ cups/480 g) of the starter. Stir in the bread flour and water to feed the remaining starter. Cover loosely and let stand at room temperature until doubled, about 4 hours. Refrigerate until ready to use. If you aren't able to feed the starter once a week (let's say that you will be on vacation), then have someone do it for you. You can occasionally extend the period between feedings to 2 weeks, but don't make a habit of it, or the starter could become too sour to use.

STARTER AND LEVAIN

Levain is a mixture of flour, water, and starter (also called culture) that is used to make a dough rise. It creates bread with an open, moist crumb.

You can make the starter in a glass or ceramic bowl and cover it with plastic wrap. However, you want a permanent and convenient home for your starter, and a plastic storage container, available at restaurant supply shops, is perfect. Choose a container that's relatively transparent, so you can see how the starter is behaving by checking its level for rising and by the network of bubbles visible through the container's sides.

To keep unwanted yeast and bacteria out of your culture, use very clean utensils, containers, and hands when mixing. In spite of your best efforts, you may catch some unpleasant yeast or bacteria in the culture. Signs are a funky aroma (as opposed to a sharp, tart, or cheeselike aroma, similar to yogurt), pink liquid on the culture's surface, or signs of mold. If you have any of these indicators, throw out the culture and start again with very clean utensils and hands.

The perfect temperature for fermenting starter is 70°F/21°C. If your kitchen is cooler or warmer, put the dough in a warm space (see page 61) or refrigerate for an hour or two, as needed. The ideal timing for feeding is in 24-hour increments so the culture has a chance to develop flavor before you feed it again. Feed the culture at the same time every day.

As the refrigerated starter is stored, it will give off a grayish liquid as a by-product of fermentation. Often called hooch, it should be stirred into the starter before feeding.

Our recipe makes about 3 cups/960 g of starter, and if you love baking artisan breads as much as we do, it may not be an excessive amount. While the Pain au Levain (page 49) uses only 1 Tbsp, the Whole-Wheat Harvest Bread (page 52) takes ½ cup/160 g. If the starter container simply takes up too much room in your refrigerator, discard (or share) half, store the remaining starter, and feed with ⅔ cup/95 g flour and ⅓ cup/75 ml water to maintain this smaller amount.

THE MODEL BAKERY ON BREAD

There are two important components of great bread: The first is high-quality organic bread flour (see page 21); the second is time. Most of this time doesn't include actual labor, only waiting. A slow rise encourages enzyme and bacterial growth, which develop flavor.

Temperature is another important factor in bread making. The ideal temperature for bread dough fermentation is 77°F/25°C. (Fermentation is another way to say "dough rising." It's a more accurate term because not all dough rises to a visibly puffed state, but in all cases, the dough creates carbon dioxide and ferments.) That means the dough should be about 77°F/25°C after mixing. You can establish the temperature of your dough with an instant-read thermometer—the flour will probably already be about this temperature, but water is usually colder.

Note that we do not use warm water (around 110°F/43°C), which is usually the recommended temperature, to make our dough. Tepid tap water works fine. But if your kitchen is cold or hot, adjust the temperature of the dough by manipulating the temperature of the mixing water. If the kitchen is cold (around 60°F/16°C), use lukewarm water. If the kitchen is hot (over 80°F/27°C), you can use ice-cold water, which is what we often do when the Valley weather is hot and the ovens are blasting.

In some cases, a pre-ferment (a previously mixed and fermented dough) is added to the dough for extra flavor and improved shelf life. Depending on the texture, a pre-ferment can also be called a biga (when stiff, like a dough) or a poolish or sponge (thinner and more batter-like). Be sure to allow the necessary time to make the pre-ferment.

Some home bakers may be unfamiliar with the new "pull and wait" technique, which professional bakers are using with more frequency to make artisan breads. Here's a brief explanation of how it works: Gluten is the component in flour that gives the dough structure, and it activates when moistened. In the past, traditional bread recipes needed to be about 60 percent hydration so the dough was dry enough to be kneaded by hand or with a mixer. (The percentage of water in the dough is called its hydration.) Wet doughs, with closer to 80 percent hydration, bake into crusty loaves with chewy, airy interiors, but they are too wet to knead in the traditional manner. It was discovered that pulling at the dough a few times over the course of an hour works as well for developing gluten as 10 minutes of kneading by hand. And as the wet dough rests, the flour absorbs the water, so that the dough can be shaped into a loaf. We utilize this method to make our pain au levain.

For drier doughs, we use a mixer. When using a stand mixer, attach the paddle blade and mix the dough ingredients just until they are combined. Hold back some of the flour to allow for variations in the ambient humidity. Cover the mixer bowl with a kitchen towel and let the dough rest for about 20 minutes. This is called the autolyse; it allows the dry ingredients to absorb the water, so you don't have to add too much flour at the next step. Now mix in enough additional flour to make a dough with the consistency described in the recipe. At this point, switch from the paddle to the dough hook and mix on medium-low speed, adding a sprinkle of flour if the dough sticks excessively to the bowl. In most cases, you want a smooth finished dough that remains tacky but isn't sticky to the touch.

During kneading, some soft doughs will "climb" up the dough hook. If allowed to stay there, the texture of the dough will be compromised. Just stop the machine, pull the dough down and back into the bowl, and resume kneading. You may have to do this three or four times.

If you prefer to knead dough by hand, stir the dough ingredients in a large bowl, adding just enough flour so the dough becomes too dense to stir. Cover and let stand for 10 minutes. Turn the dough out onto a floured work surface and knead, adding more flour as necessary, to make a dough of the desired consistency. Kneading is simple: Fold a quarter of the dough over to the center of the mass and press it down. Rotate the dough a quarter turn, fold another quarter of the dough over, and press again. Repeat the process—you will get into a relaxing rhythm—until the dough is smooth, tacky to the touch, and springs back into place when pulled gently (this is what is meant by "elastic dough"), 8 to 10 minutes.

 If you are not sure if your hand- or machine-kneaded dough has been kneaded long enough, use the window-pane test. This simple technique indicates that the gluten has been sufficiently activated and strengthened. Tear off a golf ball–size piece of dough and flatten it into a square. Gently pull the dough on all four sides to make a larger, thinner square. If you can pull the dough into a membrane-like thickness without tearing, the dough is ready. If it tears readily, knead longer.

 Once the dough is mixed, it often requires a warm place of about 77°F/25°C to ferment, the period when the dough's flavor develops. In most houses, warm places include a spot near a radiator or hot water heater (but not on them, which would be too hot). A turned-off gas oven with a light bulb burning works well. If you have an electric oven, turn the oven on for no more than a minute, and then turn it off before putting the container of dough inside. A large microwave oven with a glass of steaming hot water placed next to the container of dough also works. If the dough is fermenting in an oven, remember not to turn on the oven while it is holding the dough!

Proofing is the period after fermentation when the shaped dough is allowed to expand before baking. (Some people also use the term to describe the process of dissolving yeast in warm liquid to check—or prove—its potency, but with instant yeast, that process is going the way of the dinosaur.) Depending on the recipe, the dough may or may not double in volume. To check whether the dough has proofed enough, push a floured fingertip about 1 in/2.5 cm into the dough. It should leave an impression that fills in very slowly.

A banneton is a cloth-lined wicker (or sometimes plastic) basket used to hold the dough during its final fermentation. (It is sometimes called a bread mold or basket, or by its German name, *Brotform*.) Wet dough, such as pain au levain, would spread without the basket to contain it. If you're a serious home baker, you will want to own a banneton or two, but you can easily improvise with a smallish (about 8 in/20 cm in diameter) colander. The colander holes simulate the open weave of the wicker banneton.

 Many bread cookbooks now recommend baking the shaped loaf on a baking stone covered by a hot pot. The pot traps the steam given off by the baking bread, and the extra moisture helps create a thick crust. The proximity of the hot pot to the dough simulates the intense, close heat of a professional oven and encourages deep browning, yielding a crusty loaf. That's all good, but a cast-iron pot is very heavy and difficult to handle, especially when heated to 500°F/260°C/gas 10. For baking at home, we use a 6-qt/5.7-L aluminum metal pot (the one we use to boil water for pasta), and it works very well. Even a roasting pan will work. Be sure the pot has metal handles and can withstand high heat (500°F/260°C/ gas 10). Use a relatively heavy pot, but an inexpensive one, and certainly one with heat-resistant handles. You may want to reserve a pot for baking bread, as the oven heat may eventually discolor the surface. If you want to use a cast-iron pot, it's your choice.

YEASTED
SWEETS

On Karen's first trip to Europe, of all the things she ate that were new experiences, the flaky yeasted pastries of France impressed her the most. Hardly any American bakeries were making croissants, much less ones filled with almond paste or chocolate, and Danish (called *viennoiserie* in French, because it was Viennese bakers who popularized these baked goods in Europe) were restricted to just a few shapes. She swore that one day she would learn how to make these fabulous creations, and when she did, it was with an enormous sense of accomplishment. You will have the same satisfaction when you bring these home-made delights, freshly baked in your own oven, to the breakfast table.

CROISSANTS

MAKES 16 CROISSANTS

One of the joys of home baking is being able to make some of your favorites from your local bakery, and even improve on them. There are many commercially made croissants that resemble dinner rolls and even cakes instead of the flaky French masterpieces. But this recipe makes croissants identical to the ones you would get at a fine bakery in Paris (or St. Helena!)—shatteringly crisp on the outside, pleasantly chewy and buttery on the inside.

---

1 recipe Croissant Dough (page 80)

Unbleached all-purpose flour for rolling the dough

1 large egg yolk

1 Tbsp heavy cream or milk

1. Place the dough on a lightly floured work surface with the long open seam facing you (look carefully) and the fold facing away from you. Cut the dough in half vertically, so you end up with two portions with open seams. Leave one of them, long side facing you, on the work surface, and lightly flour the top of the dough. Refrigerate the other portion of dough.

2. Using a large, heavy rolling pin, roll out the dough into a 12-by-8-in/30.5-by-20-cm rectangle, with the long side facing you. If the dough retracts, cover it with a kitchen towel and let it relax for 5 minutes before rolling again. Pull the lower left corner of the dough out about 2 in/5 cm to the left to make a 45-degree angle. Pull the upper right corner out to make a 45-degree angle on that side of the dough, creating a parallelogram with two 14-in-/35.5-cm-long sides.

3. Starting at the bottom left corner of the dough, mark the dough with the tip of a knife at 3½-in/9-cm intervals along the base (see photo 1, page 66). Starting at the upper left corner of the dough, repeat, making

notches along the top at 3½-in/9-cm intervals as well. Using a ruler, starting at the upper left corner of the dough, connect the top and bottom notches with diagonal lines, and score lightly with the tip of the knife. Using a sharp knife, cut along the lines to make eight triangles, 8 in/20 cm high and 3½ in/9 cm wide at the base (see photo 2, page 66). Cut a 1-in/2.5-cm vertical notch in the center of each triangle base (see photo 3, page 66). Set the triangles aside. Repeat with the remaining dough.

4. Line two half-sheet pans with parchment paper. To shape each croissant, gently stretch the base of the triangle until it is about 5 in/12 cm wide. Holding the triangle at its base, stretch the triangle from its tip until the triangle is about 10 in/25 cm tall.

5. Starting from the base, roll up the triangle (see photo 4, page 66). Curve the croissant into a tight crescent and press the pointed ends together. Place the croissant, with the tip of the triangle underneath the pastry, on one of the lined pans. Repeat with the remaining triangles, putting eight

CONTINUED

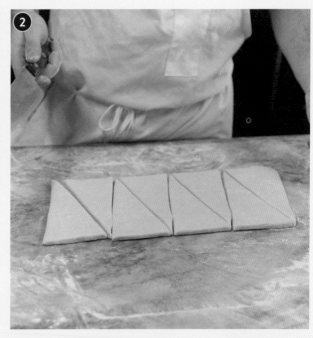

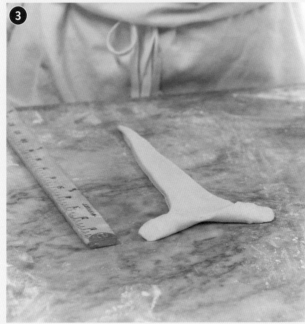

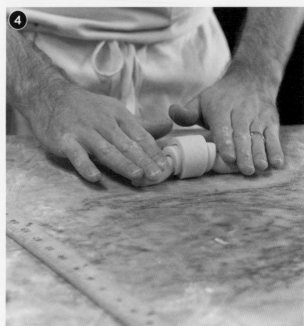

croissants on each pan and spacing them well apart. Cover each pan loosely with plastic wrap and let stand in a warm place until the croissants look puffed, about 1½ hours.

6. Position racks in the top third and center of the oven and preheat to 400°F/ 200°C/gas 6.

7. Beat the egg yolk and cream together in a small bowl. Brush the tops of the croissants lightly with the glaze.

8. Bake until golden brown, about 20 minutes, switching the pans from top to bottom and front to back halfway through baking. Transfer to a wire cooling rack and let cool for at least 20 minutes. Serve warm or at room temperature. (Cooled croissants can be stored in an airtight container at room temperature for up to 1 day.)

ALMOND CROISSANTS

MAKES 16 CROISSANTS

A variation on the croissant theme, these pastries are rolled around almond filling before baking. Unlike classic croissants, we do not curve these into crescents, but bake them into straight pastries. When buying almond paste, don't mix it up with marzipan, which is much sweeter.

ALMOND FILLING

⅓ cup plus 1 Tbsp/115 g packed almond paste, crumbled

2 tsp sugar

Pinch of fine sea salt

4 Tbsp/55 g unsalted butter, at room temperature

1 large egg yolk

1 Tbsp plus 1 tsp unbleached all-purpose flour

1 recipe Croissant Dough (page 80)

1 large egg yolk

1 Tbsp heavy cream or milk

¼ cup/30 g sliced almonds

Confectioners' sugar for dusting

1. **TO MAKE THE FILLING:** Process the almond paste, sugar, and salt in a food processor fitted with the metal blade until the almond paste is very finely chopped. Add the butter, egg yolk, and flour and pulse until smooth. Transfer to a bowl, cover with plastic wrap, and refrigerate until firm enough to spread, at least 1 hour or up to 1 day.

2. Line two half-sheet pans with parchment paper. Follow the recipe for croissants through step 3, but do not cut a slit in the triangle base. About ¼ in/6 mm from the bottom of the triangle, spread about 2½ tsp of filling in a wide strip. Starting from the base, roll up the triangle, enclosing the filling. Place the croissant, with the tip of the triangle underneath the pastry, on one of the lined pans. Repeat with the remaining triangles, putting eight croissants on each pan and spacing them well apart. Cover each pan loosely with plastic wrap and let stand in a warm place until the croissants look puffed, about 1½ hours.

3. Position racks in the top third and center of the oven and preheat to 400°F/ 200°C/gas 6.

4. Beat the egg yolk and cream together in a small bowl. Brush the tops of the croissants lightly with the glaze and sprinkle with the sliced almonds.

5. Bake until golden brown, about 20 minutes, switching the pans from top to bottom and front to back halfway through baking. Transfer to a wire cooling rack and let cool for at least 20 minutes. Dust with confectioners' sugar and serve warm or at room temperature. (Cooled croissants can be stored in an airtight container at room temperature for up to 1 day.)

PAINS AU CHOCOLAT

MAKES 12 CROISSANTS

Any day that starts out with chocolate is bound to be a good one, and *pain au chocolat*, chocolate-stuffed croissant pastry, lives up to this premise. Bakeries buy specially made chocolate sticks called batons to put inside the dough. They are available online, but standard chocolate bars can also be cut into strips for the same purpose. This is one case where the cacao content is immaterial, so just use your favorite brand.

Three 3½-oz/100-g semisweet or bittersweet chocolate bars

1 recipe Croissant Dough (page 80)

Unbleached all-purpose flour for rolling out the dough

1 large egg yolk

1 Tbsp heavy cream

1. Let the chocolate bars stand in a warm place for 10 minutes or so. They must be slightly warm so they cut cleanly and do not shatter. Cut each bar crosswise into eight equal strips for a total of twenty-four.

2. Line two half-sheet pans with parchment paper. Place the dough on a lightly floured work surface. Lightly flour the top of the dough. Using a large, heavy rolling pin, roll out the dough into a 20-by-15-in/50-by-38-cm rectangle. If the dough retracts, cover it with a kitchen towel and let it relax for 5 minutes before rolling again.

3. Using a yardstick and a sharp knife, cut the dough into twelve 5-in/12-cm squares. For each pain au chocolat, place a square in front of you. Place a chocolate strip about ½ in/12 mm up from the bottom of the square. Fold the bottom of the square over the chocolate strip to enclose it. Place a second chocolate strip above the first one and roll up the square. Pinch the long seam

closed. Place on one of the lined pans, seam-side down. Continue with the remaining dough squares and chocolate strips, putting six pastries on each pan, about 2 in/5 cm apart. Cover each pan loosely with plastic wrap and let stand in a warm place until the pastries look puffed, about 1½ hours.

4. Position racks in the top third and center of the oven and preheat to 400°F/200°C/gas 6.

5. Beat the egg yolk and cream together in a small bowl. Brush the tops of the pastries lightly with the glaze. Bake until golden brown, 20 to 25 minutes, switching the pans from top to bottom and front to back halfway through baking. Transfer to a wire cooling rack and let cool for at least 20 minutes. Serve warm or at room temperature. (Cooled pains au chocolat can be stored in an airtight container at room temperature for up to 1 day.)

BEAR CLAWS

MAKES 12 BEAR CLAWS

One doesn't see many recipes for bear claws, a Danish pastry classic that we bake daily. The almond-flavored filling uses cake crumbs for the base, so gather them up from yellow or white cake trimmings, or buy a couple of unfrosted cupcakes at your local bakery. We can guarantee that your friends will be surprised when they find out that these were baked in your oven.

FILLING

¾ cup/85 g sliced almonds

⅔ cup/55 g sweetened shredded coconut

⅓ cup/65 g sugar

⅓ cup/105 g packed almond paste, crumbled

1 cup/100 g vanilla-flavored cake crumbs

3 Tbsp unsalted butter, at room temperature

1 large egg yolk

1 recipe Croissant Dough (page 80)

Unbleached all-purpose flour for rolling out the dough

1 large egg yolk

1 Tbsp heavy cream or milk

¼ cup/30 g sliced almonds

Confectioners' sugar for dusting

1. **TO MAKE THE FILLING**: Process the almonds, coconut, and sugar in a food processor fitted with the metal blade until the almonds are very finely chopped. Add the almond paste and pulse until processed into fine crumbs. Add the cake crumbs, butter, and egg yolk and pulse until combined. Transfer to a bowl, cover with plastic wrap, and refrigerate until firm enough to shape, at least 2 hours or up to 1 day.

2. Shape the filling into twelve logs about 5 in/12 cm long; set aside.

3. Line two half-sheet pans with parchment paper. Place the dough on a lightly floured work surface. Lightly flour the top of the dough. Using a large, heavy rolling pin, roll out the dough into a 20-by-15-in/50-by-38-cm rectangle. If the dough retracts, cover it with a kitchen towel and let it relax for 5 minutes before rolling again.

4. Using a yardstick and a sharp knife, cut the dough into twelve 5-in/12-cm squares. Place a dough square in front of you. Place one of the filling logs ¾ in/2 cm up from the bottom of the square. Fold the top of the square over just to enclose the log, leaving about ½ in/1.25 cm of dough

exposed beneath the seam, and press the seam closed. Cut three equally spaced slits in the exposed flap of dough to make four tabs for the "toes." Place the pastry on one of the lined pans, curving it into a U shape to open space between the tabs. Repeat with the remaining dough and filling. Place six pastries on each pan, spacing them well apart. Cover each pan loosely with plastic wrap and let stand in a warm place until the pastries look puffed, about 1½ hours.

5. Position racks in the top third and center of the oven and preheat to 375°F/190°C/gas 5.

6. Beat the egg yolk and cream together in a small bowl. Brush the tops of the pastries lightly with the egg mixture and sprinkle with the almonds.

7. Bake until golden brown, about 20 minutes, switching pans from top to bottom and front to back halfway through baking. Transfer to a wire cooling rack and let cool for at least 20 minutes. Dust with confectioners' sugar. Serve warm or at room temperature. (Cooled bear claws can be stored in an airtight container at room temperature for up to 1 day.)

CLASSIC CHEESE DANISH

MAKES 12 DANISH

Cheese Danish has its fans at the bakery, probably because it is not as sweet as many of our other morning treats. Some customers have a ritual of Danish and coffee, and if the Danish is cheese and the newspaper is the *New York Times*, then you can be sure the customer is from the East Coast!

CREAM CHEESE FILLING

8 oz/225 g cream cheese, at room temperature

3 Tbsp sugar

Pinch of fine sea salt

1 egg yolk

½ tsp pure vanilla extract

Grated zest of ½ lemon

Grated zest of ¼ orange

1 recipe Croissant Dough (page 80)

Unbleached all-purpose flour for rolling out the dough

1 large egg yolk

1 Tbsp heavy cream or milk

APRICOT GLAZE

⅔ cup/200 g apricot jam or preserves

2 Tbsp water

1. **TO MAKE THE FILLING**: Mash the cream cheese, sugar, and salt together in a small bowl with a rubber spatula until smooth. Add the egg yolk, vanilla, and lemon and orange zests and mash until combined.

2. Line two half-sheet pans with parchment paper. Place the chilled dough on a lightly floured work surface. Lightly flour the top of the dough. Using a large, heavy rolling pin, roll out the dough into a 20-by-15-in/50-by-38-cm rectangle. If the dough retracts, cover it with a kitchen towel and let it relax for 5 minutes before rolling again.

3. Using a yardstick and a sharp knife, cut the dough into twelve 5-in/12-cm squares. Place a dough square in front of you with the points facing up, down, right, and left. Place a heaping 1 Tbsp of the filling in the center of the square. Fold the right and left points to meet over the center of the filling and pinch them together. Place the pastry on one of the lined pans. Repeat with the remaining dough and filling. Place six on each pan, spacing them well apart. Cover each pan loosely with plastic wrap and let stand in a warm place until the pastries look puffed, about 1½ hours.

4. Position racks in the top third and center of the oven and preheat to 350°F/180°C/gas 4.

5. Beat the egg yolk and cream together in a small bowl. Lightly brush the exposed dough of the pastries with the egg mixture. Bake until golden brown, 20 to 25 minutes, switching the pans from top to bottom and front to back halfway through baking. Transfer to a wire cooling rack and let cool for at least 20 minutes.

6. **TO MAKE THE GLAZE**: Bring the apricot jam and water to a brisk simmer in a small saucepan over medium heat, stirring often. Cook, continuing to stir often, until thickened, about 1 minute. When you drop some of the glaze from the spoon, the last drops should be very thick and slow to fall. Strain through a wire sieve into a small bowl.

7. Brush the pastries with the warm apricot glaze. Serve warm or at room temperature. (Cooled pastries can be stored in an airtight container at room temperature for up to 1 day.)

CHEESE AND BERRY DANISH

MAKES 16 DANISH

These look plain on the outside, but there is a surprise filling of cream cheese and seasonal berries. You can use just about any berry, although strawberries lose their color when cooked and raspberries can be a bit tart with cream cheese. The pastries are baked in muffin cups to hold their shapes.

1 recipe Croissant Dough (page 80)

Unbleached all-purpose flour for rolling out the dough

Butter, at room temperature, for the muffin cups

Cream Cheese Filling (facing page)

48 fresh berries, such as blueberries, blackberries, or huckleberries

1 large egg yolk

1 Tbsp heavy cream or milk

Confectioners' sugar for dusting

1. Place the dough on a lightly floured work surface. Lightly flour the top of the dough. Using a large, heavy rolling pin, roll out the dough into a 16-in/40.5-cm square. If the dough retracts, cover it with a kitchen towel and let it relax for 5 minutes before rolling again.

2. Using a yardstick and a sharp knife, cut the dough into sixteen 4-in/10-cm squares.

3. Lightly butter sixteen muffin cups. Fit a dough square in a muffin cup, letting the corners of the square extend beyond the cup. Fill with about 2 tsp of the filling and 3 berries. Fold the dough over to enclose the filling and pinch the seams closed. Repeat with the remaining squares of dough, filling, and berries. When all of the pastries are formed, turn them seam-side down inside the muffin cups. Cover the pans loosely with plastic wrap. Let stand in a warm place until the pastries look puffed, about 1½ hours.

4. Position a rack in the center of the oven and preheat to 375°F/190°C/gas 5.

5. Beat the egg yolk and cream together in a small bowl. Brush the tops of the pastries lightly with the egg mixture.

6. Bake until golden brown, 20 to 25 minutes. Let cool in the pans for 5 minutes. Invert the pans and unmold the pastries. Transfer to wire cooling racks and let cool for 15 minutes. Dust confectioners' sugar over the pastries. Serve warm or at room temperature. (Cooled pastries can be stored in an airtight container at room temperature for up to 1 day.)

MORNING BUNS

MAKES 12 BUNS

What could be better than freshly baked croissants? How about if we roll up the dough with a little brown sugar, slice it into buns, and, after baking, roll the warm buns in cinnamon-sugar? These have become one of the Bay Area's favorite ways to start the day, and justifiably so.

Butter, at room temperature, for the muffin cups

1 recipe Croissant Dough (page 80)

Unbleached all-purpose flour for rolling out the dough

6 Tbsp/85 g light brown sugar

2 tsp ground cinnamon

½ cup/100 g granulated sugar

1. Butter twelve muffin cups. Place the dough on a lightly floured work surface with the long open seam facing you (look carefully) and the fold facing away from you. Cut the dough in half vertically so you end up with two portions with open seams. Working with one portion at a time, with the long side still facing you, lightly flour the top of the dough.

2. Using a larger heavy rolling pin, roll out the dough into a 16-by-8-in/40.5-by-20-cm rectangle, with a long side facing you. If the dough retracts, cover it with a kitchen towel and let it relax for 5 minutes before rolling again.

3. Mix the brown sugar and 1 tsp of the cinnamon together in a small bowl. Lightly brush the dough with water. Sprinkle half of the brown sugar mixture over the dough, leaving a 1-in/2.5-cm border of dough along the bottom edge.

4. Starting at this edge, roll up the dough like a jelly roll. Using a sharp knife, cut crosswise into six equal pieces. Place each one with the cut side facing up in a muffin cup and press the dough down slightly to fit into the cup. Repeat with the remaining dough and brown sugar mixture. Cover the pan loosely with plastic wrap and let stand in a warm place until the buns look puffed but not quite doubled, about 1 hour.

5. Position a rack in the center of the oven and preheat to 350°F/180°C/gas 4.

6. Bake until the buns are golden brown and the dough in the center looks dry, 25 to 30 minutes. Let cool in the pan for 3 minutes.

7. Whisk the granulated sugar and remaining 1 tsp cinnamon together in a large bowl. Carefully turn out the buns onto the work surface. One at a time, put a bun in the bowl, carefully turn it to coat all over with the sugar mixture, and transfer to a large baking sheet. Sprinkle any remaining cinnamon-sugar over the tops of the buns. Let cool slightly. Serve warm. (Cooled buns can be stored in an airtight container at room temperature for up to 1 day. The sugar coating doesn't freeze well, so don't freeze these.)

STICKY BUNS

MAKES 12 BUNS

Some bakers know these as Philadelphia cinnamon rolls, because the recipe supposedly originated with German immigrants in that city in the 1700s. They are pretty popular in California, too. Every morning we put out tray after tray of the caramelized buns, and every morning we sell out. We also sell these as whole rings during the holiday season.

1 cup/225 g unsalted butter, plus more for the pans

1⅔ cup/330 g packed light brown sugar

1 Tbsp ground cinnamon

1 recipe Schnecken Dough (page 82)

Unbleached all-purpose flour for rolling out the dough

2½ cups/235 g chopped walnuts or pecans

1. Generously butter two 8-in/20-cm cake pans. Beat the brown sugar, butter, and cinnamon together in a medium bowl with an electric mixer on medium speed until combined.

2. Roll out the chilled dough on a lightly floured work surface into an 18-by-10-in/46-by-25-cm rectangle. Spread half of the butter mixture on the dough in a thin layer, leaving a ½-in/12-mm border on all sides. Sprinkle 1½ cups/175 g of the walnuts over the butter mixture. Starting at a long side, roll up the dough and pinch the long seam closed. Cut the dough into twelve equal slices.

3. Divide and spread the remaining butter mixture in the prepared pans. Sprinkle the remaining walnuts into the bottoms of the pans. Arrange the slices, cut-side down, in the baking pans. Cover loosely with plastic wrap. Let stand in a warm place until the buns look puffed, about 1½ hours.

4. Position a rack in the center of the oven and preheat to 350°F/180°C/gas 4.

5. Bake until the buns are golden brown and the dough near the crevices looks dry, 30 to 35 minutes. Let cool in the pans for 5 minutes. Invert the pans onto a large rimmed baking sheet to unmold the buns. Scrape any of the "sauce" from the pans over the rolls. Serve warm or at room temperature. (The buns are best the day they are baked, but may be wrapped in aluminum foil and stored at room temperature for up to 2 days. Reheat the wrapped buns in a preheated 300°F/150°C/gas 2 oven until warm, 10 to 15 minutes. The topping doesn't freeze well, so don't freeze these.)

CINNAMON ROLLS

MAKES 12 ROLLS

Everyone loves cinnamon rolls, but imagine your family and friends' reactions to homemade rolls, filling the kitchen with tantalizing, spicy aromas. We top ours with a slather of cream cheese icing. This is the classic recipe, made with raisins and walnuts, but you can mix things up with dried cranberries or currants and pecans.

ROLLS

1 cup/225 g unsalted butter, at room temperature, plus more for the pans

½ cup/100 g packed light brown sugar

2 tsp ground cinnamon

1 recipe Schnecken Dough (page 82)

Unbleached all-purpose flour for rolling out the dough

½ cup/85 g dark raisins

½ cup/55 g chopped walnuts

CREAM CHEESE ICING

2 oz/55 g cream cheese, at room temperature

2 Tbsp unsalted butter, at room temperature

½ tsp pure vanilla extract

1½ cups/175 g confectioners' sugar, sifted

2 Tbsp whole milk, as needed

1. **TO MAKE THE ROLLS:** Lightly butter two 8-in/20-cm round cake pans. Beat the butter, brown sugar, and cinnamon together in a small bowl with an electric mixer at medium speed until combined.

2. Roll out the chilled dough on a lightly floured work surface into an 18-by-10-in/46-by-25-cm rectangle. Spread the butter mixture over the dough, leaving a ½-in/12-mm border on all sides. Sprinkle the raisins and walnuts over the butter mixture.

3. Starting at a long side, roll up the dough and pinch the long seam closed. Cut the dough into twelve equal slices. Arrange the six slices, cut-side down, in each of the cake pans. Cover loosely with plastic wrap and let stand in a warm place until the rolls look puffed, about 1½ hours.

4. Position a rack in the center of the oven and preheat to 350°F/180°C/gas 4.

5. Bake until the rolls are golden brown and the dough near the crevices looks dry, 30 to 35 minutes. Let cool on the pan for 10 minutes.

6. **TO MAKE THE ICING:** Beat the cream cheese, butter, and vanilla together in a medium bowl with an electric mixer set on medium speed, scraping down the sides of the bowl often with a rubber spatula, until smooth. Reduce the mixer speed to low. Gradually mix in the confectioners' sugar. Mix in enough of the milk to give the icing a spreadable consistency.

7. Spread the icing over the warm rolls. Let cool for at least 30 minutes. Serve warm or at room temperature. (The rolls are best the day they are baked, but may be wrapped in aluminum foil and stored at room temperature for up to 2 days. Reheat the wrapped rolls in a preheated 300°F/150°C/gas 2 oven until warm, 10 to 15 minutes. The icing doesn't freeze well, so don't freeze these.)

CROISSANT DOUGH

MAKES ABOUT 2½ LB/1.2KG

It's true—you can make croissants (and other breakfast goodies based on the same dough) at home. This is an example of laminated dough: The dough is folded several times to create tissue-thin layers of dough and butter, which give the baked goods their famous flakiness. European-style butter is best for layering, as its higher butterfat content makes the dough more pliable and easier to roll into thin sheets without breaking. We provide you with lots of tips along the way, so you can have freshly baked croissants and other flaky morning time treats *chez vous.*

3⅔ cups/530 g unbleached all-purpose flour, plus more as needed

¾ cup/180 ml water

½ cup/120 ml whole milk

3 Tbsp sugar

2 Tbsp European-style or regular unsalted butter, at room temperature, thinly sliced, plus 1 cup/225 g cold butter

2 tsp instant (also called quick-rising or bread machine) yeast

1¼ tsp fine sea salt

1. At least 6 hours and up to 24 hours before baking, put the flour, water, milk, sugar, 2 Tbsp room-temperature butter, yeast, and salt in the bowl of a stand mixer. Affix the bowl to the mixer and fit with the paddle. Mix on low speed just until the dough is cohesive, adding more flour as needed. The dough should be soft and tacky to the touch, so do not add too much flour. Also, the dough will be worked during the rolling and folding process, so it is not necessary to knead it at this point. (To make by hand, combine the flour, water, milk, sugar, 2 Tbsp butter, yeast, and salt in a large bowl and mix, adding more flour as necessary, to make a rough, tacky dough.)

2. Gather up the dough and turn out onto a lightly floured work surface. Pat and shape into a 1-in-/2.5-cm-thick rectangle. Wrap the dough tightly in plastic wrap. Refrigerate for at least 2 and up to 4 hours. The dough will not rise much.

3. Beat the 1 cup/225 g cold butter in the bowl of a stand mixer fitted with the paddle attachment until it is smooth and pliable but still cool, about 2 minutes. (Or work the butter in a bowl, squeezing it between your fingers just until it is pliable; then beat with a wooden spoon or electric mixer until smooth.) The idea here is to have the dough and the butter at about the same cool temperature, as the butter must retain its texture during the rolling and folding process. If the butter is too warm, it will ooze out of the dough, and the baked croissants will be greasy and heavy.

4. Unwrap the dough and place on a lightly floured work surface. Using a long rolling pin, pummel the chilled dough to coax it into a larger rectangle measuring about 12 by 6 in/30.5 by 15 cm, with a long side facing you. Flour the top of the dough and roll it into an 18-by-10-in/46-by-25-cm rectangle. Use a lot of upper body strength to do the rolling; this isn't pie dough. Brush off the excess flour with a pastry brush.

5. Using your fingertips, starting at the left side of the dough, smear the processed butter over two-thirds of the dough, leaving the right one-third unbuttered. Fold the dough into thirds like a business letter: Fold the unbuttered section over the middle section, and then fold the buttered section over the unbuttered third. This is called a turn. Rotate the dough so the long open seam faces you. Roll out the dough again into an 18-by-10-in/46-by-25-cm rectangle. If at any time some of the butter oozes through the dough (it shouldn't, unless the kitchen is warm), sprinkle some flour over the area to seal it. Repeat the folding into thirds for a second turn, brushing excess flour off the dough as needed. Place on a small baking sheet, cover with plastic wrap, and refrigerate for 20 to 30 minutes. This brief resting period will relax the gluten and lightly chill the butter, making the dough easier to roll and keeping the butter layers from softening.

6. Unwrap the dough and place on the lightly floured work surface with the long open seam facing you. Repeat the rolling and folding for a third turn, brushing excess flour off the dough as needed. Rewrap the dough and refrigerate for at least 30 minutes or up to 18 hours before using.

SCHNECKEN DOUGH

MAKES ABOUT 2 LB/910 G

This butter-rich sweet dough is used to create familiar spiral "snail" pastries (*Schnecken* means "snails" in German), but we use it for a lot of our other Danish-style sweets, too. The idea behind schnecken dough is to make it the night before, so you can assemble and bake fresh rolls the next morning. Like croissant dough, it is much easier to handle when it is chilled, and you get great results without the lamination process that croissant dough requires.

SPONGE

½ cup/75 g unbleached all-purpose flour

¼ cup/60 ml water

¼ tsp instant (also called quick-rising or bread machine) yeast

DOUGH

⅔ cup/165 ml whole milk

2 large eggs

2 tsp instant (also called quick-rising or bread machine) yeast

1 tsp fine sea salt

3 cups/435 g bread flour, as needed

¼ cup/50 g sugar

6 Tbsp/85 g unsalted butter, at room temperature

1. **TO MAKE THE SPONGE:** The day before baking, combine the flour, water, and yeast in a small bowl. Cover with plastic wrap. Let stand in a warm place until the surface shows bubbles, about 1½ hours.

2. **TO MAKE THE DOUGH:** Combine the sponge, milk, eggs, yeast, and salt in the bowl of a stand mixer. Affix the bowl to the mixer and fit with the paddle. Mix on low speed until the sponge has dissolved. Gradually mix in 2½ cups/365 g of the flour to make a sticky dough. Turn off the mixer, cover the bowl with a kitchen towel, and let stand for 20 minutes. (To make by hand, stir the sponge, milk, eggs, yeast, and salt in a large bowl. Stir in enough of the flour to make a shaggy dough. Cover and let stand.)

3. Mix the dough on medium-low speed, gradually adding the sugar. Mix in enough of the remaining flour to make a soft dough that cleans the sides of the bowl. Replace the paddle with the dough hook. Knead on medium-low speed until smooth and elastic, about 8 minutes. Add the butter, 1 Tbsp

at a time, letting the dough absorb each addition before adding the next. Knead until the dough is shiny, about 1 minute more. Turn out the dough onto a lightly floured work surface. (To make by hand, sprinkle 1 Tbsp of the sugar over the dough in the bowl. Using floured hands, pull up about one-third of the dough, stretching it about 10 in/25 cm, and fold over the top of the dough. Flip the dough over and repeat with another 1 Tbsp sugar. Repeat twice more, flipping the dough and working in the remaining sugar. Turn the dough out onto a floured work surface. Knead, adding more flour as necessary, until the dough is supple, about 8 minutes. Dot the dough with 1 Tbsp of butter and continue kneading until the butter is absorbed. The dough will feel sticky, but do not add too much flour to compensate. Repeat with the remaining butter, kneading until the dough is smooth and shiny.)

4. Shape the dough into a thick rectangle. Wrap well in plastic wrap and refrigerate for at least 8 hours or up to 24 hours before using. The dough will look puffy, but not doubled.

THE MODEL BAKERY ON YEASTED SWEETS

These recipes are shaped a bit smaller than the ones at the bakery. This way, you can make a batch of the croissant or schnecken dough, make them into assorted shapes with various folds and fillings, and offer a wonderful selection at a special brunch or holiday breakfast.

Do not try to make the basic croissant or schnecken dough in smaller amounts. Each recipe makes between 2¼ lb/1.3 kg and 2½ lb/1.2 kg of dough. It is better to make the pastries and freeze them, unbaked, and then defrost and bake as needed. You can also freeze baked pastries (see Freezing Baked Goods, page 112).

These are sturdy doughs, so allow plenty of room for rolling, and use a long (16 in/40.5 cm or more), heavy rolling pin and lots of upper body strength. If you have an average-size kitchen counter, clear off all of the appliances to give yourself elbow room. Or you may want to work on a large pastry board set on a table. To measure and cut the dough into precise portions, a yardstick and a sharp knife will come in handy.

The croissant and schnecken doughs are easiest to work with when chilled. If you want to bake these pastries for breakfast or brunch, roll, cut, and shape the chilled dough in the morning and allow it to rise before baking. Do not refrigerate the dough for longer than 24 hours, or it could develop a fermented, slightly sour flavor. Both doughs can be double-wrapped in plastic wrap and aluminum foil and frozen for up to 2 weeks. Defrost for about 18 hours in the refrigerator before using.

You will also need plenty of space for the pastries to rise on their pans. A warm oven (see page 61) is a good place to get them out of your way, but don't forget to remove them before you preheat the oven for baking.

BREAKFAST
FAVORITES

Here is a collection of some of our bestselling baked goods; they will be just as popular in your home as they are at the bakery. While the yeasted sweets in this book are masterpieces of the baker's art and admittedly require a bit of practice, the recipes in this chapter are ones that you can make when you are half awake in the morning. They require no advance planning. The common name for this category of baked goods is quick breads, and they are, indeed, quick to make, and to disappear from the breakfast table!

THE MODEL BAKERY'S
GRANOLA

MAKES ABOUT 3½ QT/1.6 KG

Our granola has become one of our signature items; it is known throughout the Valley for its generous spicing, rich honey flavor, and abundant nuts. The beauty of making granola at home is personalizing it to your taste. If you don't like coconut, leave it out. Or substitute cashews for the walnuts, and other dried fruits (such as chopped apricots or dates) for the raisins. Consider giving a big jar of your homemade granola to some lucky recipient as a thank-you or holiday gift. If you wish, serve it like we do at the bakery, layered as a parfait with fresh berries and plain yogurt.

6 cups/510 g old-fashioned (rolled) oats

1⅓ cups/150 g sliced almonds

⅔ cup/90 g shelled sunflower seeds

⅔ cup/70 g shelled pumpkin seeds

⅔ cup/75 g coarsely chopped walnuts

⅔ cup/75 g coarsely chopped pecans

1 tsp ground allspice

1 tsp ground cinnamon

1 tsp ground cloves

1 tsp freshly grated nutmeg

1 tsp fine sea salt

½ cup/120 ml vegetable oil

½ cup/120 ml honey, such as amber, orange blossom, or eucalyptus

1½ cups/255 g golden or dark raisins

1 cup/85 g sweetened shredded coconut

1 cup/170 g dried cranberries

1. Position racks in the top third and center of the oven and preheat to 325°F/165°C/gas 3.

2. Combine the oats, almonds, sunflower seeds, pumpkin seeds, walnuts, and pecans in a very large bowl. Mix the allspice, cinnamon, cloves, nutmeg, and salt together in a small bowl. Sprinkle over the oat mixture and mix. Whisk the vegetable oil and honey together in a medium bowl, drizzle over the oat mixture, and mix again.

3. Divide the oat mixture between two half-sheet pans and spread out evenly. Bake, stirring occasionally and switching pans from top to bottom and front to back halfway through baking, until the granola is fragrant and just beginning to toast, about 30 minutes.

4. Remove from the oven. Divide the raisins, coconut, and cranberries among the baking sheets and stir to combine. Let cool completely. The granola can be stored in airtight containers at room temperature for up to 2 weeks.

THE MODEL BAKERY COOKBOOK

BUTTERMILK BISCUITS

It was Karen's grandmother Stella who taught her how to make these flaky biscuits, which fly out of the bread basket. She said that her secret was a touch of sugar. That may be true, but handling the dough with a light hand is also essential, as is the combination of buttermilk as a tenderizer and half-and-half as an enrichment. Stella would be proud to know that, every day, dozens of her biscuits grace many tables in the Valley. One year, we served miniature biscuits with homemade jams at Auction Napa Valley. Their wholesome goodness made them a hit, even though they were offered alongside fancier fare from the best restaurants around.

---

3 cups/435 g unbleached all-purpose flour, plus more for rolling out the dough

2½ tsp baking powder

½ tsp baking soda

½ tsp sugar

½ tsp fine sea salt

¾ cup/170 g cold unsalted butter, cut into ½-in/12-mm pieces

¾ cup/180 ml buttermilk

½ cup/120 ml half-and-half, plus more for brushing the biscuits

1. Position a rack in the center of the oven and preheat to 400°F/200°C/gas 6. Line a large rimmed baking sheet with parchment paper.

2. Sift the flour, baking powder, baking soda, sugar, and salt together into a medium bowl. Add the butter and toss to coat with the flour mixture. Using a pastry blender or two knives, cut in the butter until the mixture is crumbly, with some pea-size pieces of butter. Whisk the buttermilk and half-and-half together. Make a well in the center of the flour mixture and add the buttermilk mixture. Stir to thoroughly moisten the dry ingredients, including any crumbly bits in the bottom of the bowl. (You may not use all of the liquid.) Knead the dough in the bowl just a few times, until it comes together into a moist dough.

3. Turn out the dough onto a floured work surface. Dust the top with flour. Pat or roll the dough about ¾ in/2 cm thick. Using a biscuit cutter 2½ in/6 cm in diameter, cut out biscuits and place them 1 in/2.5 cm apart on the lined baking sheet. Gather up the scraps, gently knead together, and repeat, cutting out more biscuits until the dough is used up. Brush the tops of the biscuits lightly with half-and-half.

4. Bake until the biscuits are golden brown on the top and bottom (lift up a biscuit to check), 20 to 25 minutes. Serve warm. (The biscuits are best the day they are baked.)

CRANBERRY BUTTERMILK SCONES

MAKES 8 LARGE SCONES

In Britain, a scone is a scone is a scone. There isn't much gilding of the lily. Leave it to American ingenuity to flavor scones. This version's citrus goes well with a hot cup of Earl Grey tea. We love the way the slightly tart dried cranberries contrast with the sweetness of the scone.

---

3 cups/380 g unbleached all-purpose flour, plus more for the pan

½ cup/100 g granulated sugar

2½ tsp baking powder

½ tsp baking soda

¾ tsp fine sea salt

1 cup/225 g cold unsalted butter, cut into ½-in/12-mm cubes

⅔ cup/115 g dried cranberries

Grated zest of 1 orange

1 cup plus 2 tbsp/270 ml buttermilk, plus more for brushing (optional)

2 Tbsp fresh orange juice

2 Tbsp heavy cream or milk

1 Tbsp coarse sanding sugar or granulated sugar (optional)

1. Position a rack in the center of the oven and preheat to 400°F/200°C/gas 6. Flour the bottom of an 8-in/20-cm round cake pan. Line a half-sheet pan with parchment paper.

2. Sift the flour, granulated sugar, baking powder, baking soda, and salt into a large bowl. Add the butter and toss to coat with the flour mixture. Using a pastry blender or two knives, cut in the butter until the mixture is crumbly, with some pea-size pieces of butter. Add the cranberries and orange zest and stir to coat. Whisk the buttermilk and orange juice together. Make a well in the center of the flour mixture and add the buttermilk mixture. Stir to thoroughly moisten the dry ingredients, including any crumbly bits at the bottom of the bowl. Knead the dough in the bowl just a few times, until it comes together into a moist dough.

3. Transfer the dough to the prepared pan. Using floured hands, pat the dough evenly into the pan. Invert the dough onto a floured work surface. Using a sharp knife, cut the dough into eight equal wedges. Transfer the wedges, floured-side down, to the lined pan, placing them 2 in/5 cm apart. Lightly brush each scone with the cream or additional buttermilk and sprinkle with the sanding sugar.

4. Bake until the scones are golden brown, about 25 minutes. Let cool for 5 minutes. Serve warm. (The scones can be stored in an airtight container at room temperature for up to 2 days.)

APRICOT-PECAN SCONES

MAKES 8 LARGE SCONES

These are the tender, melt-in-your-mouth scones of yore. One reason for their light texture is that they are cut from a single round into wedges, so there are no scraps to reroll, as is common with cut-out round scones. (The second batch, made from the scraps, is always tougher than the first one.) When cutting in the butter, keep it somewhat chunky, and don't overhandle the dough.

---

3 cups/380 g unbleached all-purpose flour, plus more for the pan

⅓ cup/65 g sugar

2½ tsp baking powder

½ tsp baking soda

¾ tsp fine sea salt

1 cup/225 g cold unsalted butter, cut into ½-in/12-mm cubes

⅔ cup/110 g diced dried apricots (½-in/12-mm dice)

½ cup/55 g coarsely chopped pecans, plus 2 Tbsp finely chopped pecans

Grated zest of 1 orange

1¼ cups/300 ml cold buttermilk, plus more for brushing (optional)

2 Tbsp heavy cream

1. Position a rack in the center of the oven and preheat to 400°F/200°C/gas 6. Flour the bottom of an 8-in/21-cm round cake pan. Line a half-sheet pan with parchment paper.

2. Sift the flour, sugar, baking powder, baking soda, and salt into a large bowl. Add the butter and toss to coat with the flour mixture. Using a pastry blender or two knives, cut in the butter until the mixture is crumbly, with some pea-size pieces of butter. Add the apricots, coarsely chopped pecans, and orange zest and stir to coat. Make a well in the center of the flour mixture and pour in the buttermilk. Stir to thoroughly moisten the dry ingredients, including any crumbly bits at the bottom of the bowl. Knead the dough in the bowl just a few times, until it comes together into a moist dough.

3. Turn out the dough onto a lightly floured work surface. The dough may look a little rough, but try to resist the temptation to knead it unless it is really shaggy. In that case, use just a few folds to smooth it out.

Using floured hands, pat the dough into the prepared pan. Invert the dough onto a floured work surface. Using a sharp knife, cut the dough into eight equal wedges. Transfer the wedges, floured-side down, to the lined pan, spacing them 2 in/5 cm apart. Lightly brush each scone with the cream or additional buttermilk and sprinkle with the finely chopped pecans.

4. Bake until the scones are golden brown, about 25 minutes. Let cool for 5 minutes. Serve warm. (The scones can be stored in an airtight container at room temperature for up to 2 days.)

NOTE: *If you have a busy weekend coming up and it includes houseguests, freeze the unbaked scones. Place the wedges on a parchment paper–lined baking sheet, cover tightly with plastic wrap, and freeze for up to 2 weeks. When you're ready to bake, transfer the frozen wedges to another parchment paper–lined baking sheet and bake in a preheated 425°F/220°C/gas 7 oven until golden brown, about 30 minutes.*

CREAM CURRANT SCONES

MAKES 8 LARGE SCONES

These are the classic cream scones that are served at teatime in Britain. Heavy cream makes them so rich that you don't need to serve them with clotted cream or butter, which leaves more room for our house-made lemon curd (page 162). Like our other scones, these are especially tender and flaky. Try to serve them while they're still warm from the oven.

3¾ cups/545 g unbleached all-purpose flour, plus more for the pan

1¾ cups/420 ml heavy cream, plus 2 Tbsp for brushing the scones

1 large egg

⅓ cup/65 g granulated sugar

2 Tbsp baking powder

¾ tsp fine sea salt

9 Tbsp/130 g cold unsalted butter, cut into ½-in/12-mm cubes

1 cup/170 g dried currants

1 Tbsp coarse sanding sugar or granulated sugar (optional)

1. Position a rack in the center of the oven and preheat to 400°F/200°C/gas 6. Flour an 8 in-/20-cm round cake pan. Line a half-sheet pan with parchment paper.

2. Whisk the 1½ cups/360 ml heavy cream and egg together in a small bowl. Sift the flour, granulated sugar, baking powder, and salt together into a large bowl. Add the butter and toss to coat with the flour mixture. Using a pastry blender or two knives, cut in the butter until the mixture is crumbly, with some pea-size pieces of butter. Add the currants and stir to coat. Make a well in the center of the flour mixture and add the cream mixture. Stir just until the dough holds together. Do not overmix. The dough will be sticky.

3. Transfer the dough to the prepared pan. Using floured hands, pat the dough evenly into the pan. Invert the dough onto the floured work surface. Using a sharp knife, cut the dough into eight equal wedges. Transfer the wedges to the lined pan, placing them 2 in/5 cm apart. Lightly brush each scone with the remaining cream and sprinkle with the sanding sugar. Bake until the scones are golden brown, 20 to 25 minutes. Let cool in the pan for 5 minutes. Serve warm. (The scones can be stored in an airtight container at room temperature for up to 2 days.)

THE MODEL BAKERY COOKBOOK

BLUEBERRY MUFFINS

MAKES 12 MUFFINS

Although blueberries are a summer fruit in California, frozen berries are excellent, and we make these muffins throughout the year. Having a tender, cakey blueberry muffin is a must for a successful bakery, and ours do not disappoint. Rather than fold the berries into the batter, it is better to sprinkle them into the batter-filled cups, so you get a reliable amount of fruit in each muffin. Sprinkle the berries in the center of the dough, because if they touch the metal pan during baking, they can discolor or burst.

2½ cups/365 g unbleached all-purpose flour

2 tsp baking powder

¾ tsp fine sea salt

1 cup plus 3 Tbsp/235 g sugar

5 Tbsp/70 g unsalted butter, at room temperature

¼ cup/60 ml vegetable oil

2 large eggs, at room temperature

1½ tsp pure vanilla extract

½ cup/120 ml buttermilk

1¼ cups/170 g fresh or frozen blueberries

1. Position a rack in the center of the oven and preheat to 375°F/190°C/gas 5. Line twelve standard muffin cups with paper liners.

2. Sift the flour, baking powder, and salt together into a medium bowl. Beat the sugar and butter together in a medium bowl with a hand-held electric mixer set on high speed until sandy and light in color, about 2 minutes. Gradually beat in the vegetable oil, scraping down the sides of the bowl with a rubber spatula. One at a time, beat in the eggs, followed by the vanilla. (To make by hand, beat the sugar and butter together in a large bowl with a wooden spoon until sandy and light in color, about 5 minutes. Gradually whisk in the oil. One at a time, whisk in the eggs, followed by the vanilla.) Reduce the mixer speed to low, add the flour mixture in thirds, alternating them with two equal additions of the buttermilk and mixing until just combined after each addition.

3. Using a number-16 food-portion scoop with about a ¼-cup/60-ml capacity, transfer half of the batter to the lined muffin cups, filling each cup only half full. Place 3 or 4 blueberries into each muffin cup. Divide the remaining batter among the cups, and top each one with 3 or 4 more blueberries.

4. Bake until the muffins are golden brown and the tops spring back when pressed lightly with a finger, 25 to 30 minutes. Let cool in the pan for 5 minutes. Remove from the pan, transfer to a wire cooling rack, and let cool. The muffins can be stored in an airtight container at room temperature for up to 1 day.

BANANA-WALNUT MUFFINS

MAKES 9 MUFFINS

When you don't know what to do with leftover bananas, these muffins will come to the rescue. Use yellow bananas with some brown spots on the skin; the bananas should yield easily to squeezing. Bananas that are too green will be too bland, while black-ripe ones will give the muffins an off flavor. You can mash the bananas and freeze to use later, if you prefer.

1½ cups/220 g unbleached all-purpose flour

¾ tsp baking soda

¼ tsp baking powder

½ tsp fine sea salt

1 cup/200 g sugar

¼ cup/60 ml vegetable oil

½ tsp fresh lemon juice

1 large egg, at room temperature

1 cup/225 g mashed ripe bananas

½ cup/55 g chopped walnuts, plus 2 Tbsp

1. Position a rack in the center of the oven and preheat to 375°F/190°C/gas 5. Line nine standard muffin cups with paper liners.

2. Sift the flour, baking soda, baking powder, and salt together into a medium bowl. Beat the sugar, vegetable oil, and lemon juice together in a medium bowl with a hand-held electric mixer set on high speed until pale, about 1 minute. Beat in the egg. (To make by hand, whisk the sugar, oil, and lemon juice together in a medium bowl until very pale, about 3 minutes. Whisk in the egg.) Reduce the mixer speed to low. Add the flour mixture in thirds, alternating them with two equal additions of the mashed bananas. Scrape down the sides of the bowl as needed and mix until smooth. Stir in the ½ cup/55 g walnuts.

3. Using a number-16 food-portion scoop with about a ¼-cup/60-ml capacity, transfer the batter to the lined muffin cups, filling them about three-quarters full. Divide the remaining 2 Tbsp walnuts over the tops.

4. Bake until the muffins are golden brown and a wooden toothpick inserted in the center of a muffin comes out clean, about 25 minutes. Let cool in the pan for 5 minutes. Remove from the pan, transfer to a wire cooling rack, and let cool. The muffins can be stored in an airtight container at room temperature for up to 1 day.

MULTIGRAIN MUFFINS

MAKES 10 MUFFINS

These are muffins that stick to your ribs, hearty with whole wheat, oats, walnuts, and dried fruits. While these have the robust appearance of typical "health food" muffins, they do include some butter for flavor. But the applesauce replaces some of the fat normally used in muffins, bringing the total fat content down.

¾ cup/95 g cake flour (not self-rising)

½ cup/75 g whole-wheat flour

1 tsp baking soda

1 tsp ground cinnamon

½ tsp fine sea salt

¾ cup/45 g coarsely crushed bran flake breakfast cereal

6 Tbsp/85 g unsalted butter, at room temperature

⅓ cup plus 1 Tbsp/85 g packed light brown sugar

2 large eggs, at room temperature

¾ tsp pure vanilla extract

¾ cup/210 g unsweetened applesauce

½ cup/55 g coarsely chopped walnuts

⅓ cup/55 g diced dried apricots (½-in/12-mm dice)

½ cup/85 g dried cranberries

¼ cup/20 g old-fashioned (rolled) oats, plus 2 Tbsp

1. Position a rack in the center of the oven and preheat to 400°F/200°C/gas 6. Line ten standard muffin cups with paper liners.

2. Sift the cake flour, whole-wheat flour, baking soda, cinnamon, and salt together into a medium bowl. Stir in the bran flakes. Beat the butter and brown sugar together in a large bowl with a hand-held electric mixer set on high speed until light in color, about 2 minutes. One at a time, beat in the eggs, followed by the vanilla. (To make by hand, beat the butter and brown sugar together in a large bowl with a wooden spoon until sandy and light in color, about 5 minutes. One at a time, whisk in the eggs, followed by the vanilla.) Reduce the mixer speed to low. Add the flour mixture in thirds, alternating them with two equal additions of the applesauce, and mixing just until combined after each addition. Stir in the walnuts, apricots, cranberries, and the ¼ cup/20 g oats.

3. Using a number-16 food-portion scoop with about a ¼-cup/60-ml capacity, transfer the batter to the lined muffin cups. Sprinkle the remaining 2 Tbsp oats over the tops.

4. Bake until the muffins are golden brown and the tops spring back when pressed lightly with a finger, about 20 minutes. Let cool in the pan for 5 minutes. Remove from the pan, transfer to a wire cooling rack, and let cool. The muffins can be stored in an airtight container at room temperature for up to 1 day.

MORNING GLORY MUFFINS

MAKES 16 MUFFINS

Morning Glory Muffins are a flavor-packed way to start the day, with carrots, apples, coconut, and raisins all playing a part. We have to make sure to have a fresh-baked batch on weekend afternoons at about two, when a cycling club stops in for a midpoint muffin break.

2½ cups/365 g unbleached all-purpose flour

1 tsp baking powder

1 tsp baking soda

¾ tsp fine sea salt

½ tsp ground cinnamon

1½ cups/210 g shredded carrots

1 Granny Smith apple, peeled, cored and shredded

1 cup/240 ml vegetable oil

1½ cups/300 g sugar

3 large eggs, at room temperature

1 tsp pure vanilla extract

⅔ cup/80 g sweetened shredded coconut, plus ¼ cup/30 g

½ cup/85 g dark raisins

1. Position a rack in the center of the oven and preheat to 400°F/200°C/gas 6. Line sixteen standard muffin cups with paper liners.

2. Sift the flour, baking powder, baking soda, salt, and cinnamon together into a medium bowl. Combine the carrots and apple in a small bowl. Beat the vegetable oil and sugar together in a large bowl with a hand-held electric mixer set on high speed until light in color, about 2 minutes. (Or whisk by hand for 2 minutes.) One at a time, add the eggs, beating well after each addition. Beat in the vanilla. Reduce the mixer speed to low. Add the flour mixture in thirds, alternating them with two equal additions of the carrot mixture and mixing just until combined after each addition. Mix in the ⅔ cup/80 g coconut and all of the raisins.

3. Using a number-16 food-portion scoop with about a ¼-cup/60-ml capacity, transfer the batter to the lined muffin cups. Sprinkle the remaining ¼ cup/30 g coconut over the tops.

4. Bake until the muffins are golden brown and a wooden toothpick inserted in the center comes out clean, about 25 minutes. Let cool in the pan for 5 minutes. Remove from the pan, transfer to wire cooling racks, and let cool. The muffins can be stored in an airtight container at room temperature for up to 1 day.

IRISH SODA BREAD

MAKES 1 LOAF

Irish soda bread is a seasonal treat—we bake hundreds of loaves around St. Patrick's Day—but it deserves to be served year-round, and we do! The traditional leavening is a combination of baking soda and buttermilk, but you get a better result by using baking powder, too. This bread will be out of the oven in less than an hour. So while it is commonly served with a corned beef dinner, it is also great for breakfast with jam and butter. Purists will like the plain version, but if your taste is like Sarah's, add the currants and caraway.

2⅓ cups/340 g unbleached all-purpose flour, plus more for the pan and top of the loaf

3 Tbsp sugar

1½ tsp baking powder

1 tsp baking soda

1 tsp fine sea salt

3 Tbsp cold unsalted butter, cut into ½-in/12-mm pieces

½ cup/70 g dried currants (optional)

1 tsp caraway seeds (optional)

1 cup plus 2 Tbsp/270 ml buttermilk, as needed

1. Position a rack in the center of the oven and preheat to 400°F/200°C/gas 6. Dust the bottom of an 8-in/20-cm round cake pan with flour.

2. Sift the flour, sugar, baking powder, baking soda, and salt together into a large bowl. Add the butter and stir to coat with the flour mixture. Using a pastry blender or two knives, cut in the butter until the mixture is crumbly, with some pea-size pieces of butter. Stir in the currants and caraway seeds (if using). Stir in enough of the buttermilk to make a moist, soft dough, being sure to moisten all of the dry bits on the bottom of the bowl. Knead in the bowl just a few times to be sure the dough comes together—this is not a smooth dough.

3. Turn out the dough onto a lightly floured work surface and shape into a ball. Sprinkle the top with at least 1 Tbsp flour to give the loaf a rustic look. Transfer to the prepared pan. Using a sharp knife, cut a shallow 4-in/10-cm wide X in the top of the dough. The X will open during baking and help the loaf bake more evenly.

4. Bake until the top is deep golden brown and the bread sounds hollow when tapped on the bottom, 35 to 40 minutes. Remove from the pan. Let cool on a wire cooling rack for 5 to 10 minutes, and serve warm. (The bread is best the day it is made.)

THE MODEL BAKERY ON BREAKFAST FAVORITES

 All of the muffins in this chapter use a standard muffin pan. Each cup measures about 2¾ in/7 cm in diameter and 1½ in/4 cm deep. Line the cups with paper liners for easy removal. We strongly recommend that you use a food-portion scoop to transfer the batter to the cups without a mess. The standard "blue handle" (also called number-16 in the United States) with about a ¼-cup/60-ml capacity is the right size and will fill each cup with the perfect amount of batter. Leave the batter mounded in the muffin cup, rather than leveling it, as that will give the muffin top an attractive dome shape.

 Many muffins are made by stirring the ingredients together to make a batter. This makes a good, but not great muffin. We prefer to cream the butter and sugar together, like a cake. The exception is the Morning Glory Muffins (page 99), which use vegetable oil as the main fat. Because of the relatively small volume of ingredients in these muffin batters, it is most convenient to whip them up with a hand-held electric mixer. The butter and sugar don't provide enough bulk to cream properly in a large stand mixer.

 Scones and biscuits have the fat cut into the flour to give them a flaky texture. You can use a pastry blender or two knives to do the job, or you can rub in the cold butter with your fingertips until the mixture looks crumbly, with some pea-size pieces of butter. The important thing here is to work quickly, as the butter should not warm up and soften.

CAKES

At the Model Bakery, our layer cakes have a very particular look. We like a triple-layer cake, as its height gives the most humble cake a celebratory appearance, and you can get more servings than from the typical double-layer version. They are based on the favorite cakes of our childhood—chocolaty devil's food, delicate white, yellow buttermilk, chunky carrot, and vibrant red velvet. Our frostings are as mouthwatering as the cakes and are loaded with the best cream cheese and butter. Unless we have a special request, we don't bake a lot of sponge or genoise cakes. They get most of their moisture and flavor from soaking in syrup, and we prefer the cake layers to be tasty themselves. We've also included some easy unfrosted cakes to serve when a simpler dessert is in order.

In this chapter, you will find our three core cakes: pastel yellow buttermilk, dark chocolate devil's food, and pristine white cake. These are the three basic cakes that we use time and again for birthday and other celebration cakes. If you like, you can use the cakes with your own favorite frosting for the special occasions (and even the not-so-special events) in your life. Each recipe makes three 8-in/20-cm layers.

ESPRESSO BUNDT CAKE

MAKES 12 SERVINGS

We have customers who can't get enough coffee. Even though Karen is a tea lover, and is rarely without a glass of iced tea within reach, we pay a lot of attention to the quality of our coffee beans and their preparation. This caffeinated Bundt cake is great any time of day, but it is especially good with a morning cup of freshly brewed coffee.

CAKE

1 cup/225 g unsalted butter, at room temperature, plus more for the pan

Unbleached all-purpose flour for the pan

3 cups/390 g cake flour (not self-rising)

1½ tsp baking powder

1½ tsp baking soda

½ tsp fine sea salt

2 cups/400 g granulated sugar

3 large eggs, at room temperature

1 tsp pure vanilla extract

2 cups/480 ml sour cream, at room temperature

½ cup/120 ml cold brewed espresso or Italian roast coffee (or 1 Tbsp instant espresso dissolved in ½ cup/120 ml boiling water)

GLAZE

1 cup/115 g confectioners' sugar, sifted

3 Tbsp brewed espresso (or 1 tsp instant espresso dissolved in 3 Tbsp boiling water), as needed

1. **TO MAKE THE CAKE:** Position a rack in the center of the oven and preheat to 350°F/180°C/gas 4. Butter the inside of a 12-cup/2.8-L fluted tube pan. Dust with all-purpose flour and tap out the excess.

2. Sift the cake flour, baking powder, baking soda, and salt together into a bowl. Beat the butter and granulated sugar together in a large bowl with an electric mixer on medium-high speed until light in color and texture, about 3 minutes (or beat by hand with a wooden spoon for about 10 minutes). Beat in the eggs, one at a time, and then the vanilla. Reduce the mixer speed to low. Add the flour mixture in thirds, alternating them with two equal additions of the sour cream, and scraping down the sides of the bowl as needed, mixing until smooth.

3. Transfer one-third of the batter to a medium bowl. Whisk in the cold espresso. Spoon half of the plain batter into the prepared pan. Top with the espresso batter, and then the remaining plain batter. Smooth the batter with a spatula.

4. Bake until a long bamboo skewer inserted in the center of the cake comes out clean, 50 minutes to 1 hour. Let cool in the pan on a wire cooling rack for 15 minutes.

5. Run a dinner knife around the inside of the pan to loosen the cake. Invert and unmold onto a wire cooling rack and let cool completely.

6. **TO MAKE THE GLAZE:** Put the confectioners' sugar in a small bowl. Whisk in enough of the espresso to make a glaze about the thickness of heavy cream.

7. Put the cake, while still on the cooling rack, over a large plate. Drizzle the glaze over the cake, letting the excess glaze drip down the sides. Let stand until the glaze sets. The cake can be stored, wrapped in plastic wrap, at room temperature for up to 3 days.

LEMON POUND CAKE

MAKES 12 SERVINGS

Every baker needs a homespun, almost plain cake that is easy to make, transport, and serve. This cake fills all of these requirements beautifully, and has the refreshingly tart flavor of lemon, to boot. We sometimes make it with lemons from Karen's backyard, usually the huge, very sour Eureka variety, and other times the floral-scented and milder Meyer lemons.

CAKE

1½ cups/340 g unsalted butter, at room temperature, plus more for the pan

Unbleached all-purpose flour for the pan

3 cups/390 g cake flour (not self-rising)

1 Tbsp baking powder

½ tsp salt

7 large eggs, at room temperature

3 Tbsp whole milk

2 cups/400 g sugar

Grated zest of 3 lemons

1 Tbsp fresh lemon juice

LEMON SYRUP

½ cup/120 ml fresh lemon juice

½ cup/100 g sugar

1. **TO MAKE THE CAKE:** Position a rack in the center of the oven and preheat to 350°F/180°C/gas 4. Butter the inside of a 12-cup/2.8-L fluted tube pan. Dust with all-purpose flour and tap out the excess.

2. Sift the cake flour, baking powder, and salt together into a medium bowl. Whisk the eggs and milk together in a large glass measuring cup or pitcher. Beat the sugar, butter, lemon zest, and lemon juice together in a large bowl with an electric mixer on medium-high speed until light in color and texture, about 3 minutes (or beat by hand for about 10 minutes). Reduce the mixer speed to low. Add the flour mixture in thirds, alternating them with two equal additions of the egg mixture, mixing after each addition until smooth and scraping down the sides of the bowl as needed. Spread evenly in the prepared pan.

3. Bake until the cake is golden brown and a long bamboo skewer inserted in the center of the cake comes out clean, 50 minutes to 1 hour. Let cool in the pan on a wire cooling rack for 15 minutes.

4. **TO MAKE THE SYRUP:** While the cake is cooling, bring the lemon juice and sugar to a boil in a nonreactive saucepan over medium heat, stirring often until the sugar dissolves.

5. Run a dinner knife around the inside of the pan to loosen the cake. Pierce the top of the cake all over with the skewer. Brush the top of the cake with about one-fourth of the syrup. Invert and unmold the cake onto a wire cooling rack. Place the cake, still on the rack, over a rimmed baking sheet. Gradually brush the remaining syrup over the warm cake. Let cool completely. The cake can be stored, wrapped in plastic wrap, at room temperature for up to 3 days.

THE MODEL BAKERY COOKBOOK

PUMPKIN GINGERBREAD CAKE

MAKES 12 SERVINGS

There are a lot of pumpkin "breads" out there, although, like this one, they are actually cakes. The flavors are downright patriotic (just try finding canned pumpkin, maple syrup, and molasses outside of the United States), and they really add up to a special autumn dessert. If you wish, stir 1 cup/170 g dried cranberries or 1 cup/115 g chopped walnuts into the finished batter, but we usually make it without any add-ins. Whipped cream flavored with a little brandy or rum is a nice accompaniment. When you are asked to bring dessert to an autumn party, this is a good option because it can be made a couple of days ahead and travels well.

¾ cup/170 g unsalted butter, at room temperature, plus more for the pan

Unbleached all-purpose flour for the pan

3½ cups/455 g cake flour (not self-rising)

1 Tbsp baking soda

2 tsp ground ginger

1 tsp ground cinnamon

¾ tsp ground allspice

¾ tsp fine sea salt

¾ cup/150 g packed light brown sugar

3 large eggs, at room temperature

One 15-oz/430-g can solid-pack pumpkin

¾ cup/180 ml grade B maple syrup (see Note)

3 Tbsp molasses (not blackstrap)

1 tsp pure vanilla extract

1. Position a rack in the center of the oven and preheat to 350°F/180°C/gas 4. Butter the inside of a 12-cup/2.8-L fluted tube pan. Dust with all-purpose flour and tap out the excess.

2. Sift the cake flour, baking soda, ginger, cinnamon, allspice, and salt together into a medium bowl. Beat the butter and brown sugar together in a large bowl with an electric mixer on medium-high speed until light in color and texture, about 3 minutes (or beat by hand for about 10 minutes). Beat in the eggs, one at a time. Gradually beat in the pumpkin, maple syrup, molasses, and vanilla and beat well. Don't worry if the mixture curdles. Reduce the mixer speed to low. Add the flour mixture in thirds, scraping down the sides of the bowl as needed. Spread evenly in the prepared pan.

3. Bake until the cake is nicely browned and a long bamboo skewer inserted in the center of the cake comes out clean, 50 minutes to 1 hour. Let cool in the pan on a wire cooling rack for 15 minutes.

4. Run a dinner knife around the inside of the pan to loosen the cake. Invert and unmold onto a wire cooling rack and let cool completely. The cake can be stored, wrapped in plastic wrap, at room temperature for up to 3 days.

NOTE: *Grade B maple syrup is darker and more strongly flavored than grade A, which makes it perfect for baking. (The grading system for maple syrup is by color, not quality, so B is not inferior to A.) It is easy to find at natural foods markets and many supermarkets and warehouse stores.*

CLASSIC CARROT CAKE

MAKES 10 TO 12 SERVINGS

Many extraneous ingredients are often added to carrot cake, including pineapple and coconut, but at the bakery, we are purists. It is one of the few cakes we make where vegetable oil, instead of butter, is the ingredient that makes the result so moist—and one of the only ones we make in double, and not triple, layers. With the cream cheese frosting, a triple-layer cake would be overkill. We decorate the top of the cake with piped carrots, created from orange- and green-tinted frosting. Because the batter doesn't have butter (which hardens when refrigerated), carrot cake can be served chilled.

CAKE

Butter, at room temperature, for the pans

2 cups/290 g unbleached all-purpose flour, plus more for the pans

2 tsp baking powder

2 tsp baking soda

2 tsp ground cinnamon

½ tsp fine sea salt

4 large eggs, at room temperature

1½ cups/300 g sugar

1½ cups/360 ml vegetable oil

3 cups/385 g shredded carrots

1 cup/115 g finely chopped walnuts

1 recipe Cream Cheese Frosting (page 136)

1½ cups/170 g finely chopped walnuts

Frosting Carrots (see facing page) or marzipan or candy carrots for decoration

1. **TO MAKE THE CAKE:** Position a rack in the center of the oven and preheat to 350°F/180°C/gas 4. Lightly butter two 8-in/20-cm round cake pans that have 2-in/5-cm sides. Line the bottoms with parchment or wax paper rounds. Dust the insides of the pans with all-purpose flour and tap out the excess.

2. Sift the flour, baking powder, baking soda, cinnamon, and salt together into a medium bowl. Beat the eggs in large bowl with an electric mixer set on high speed until foamy. Gradually beat in the sugar and continue mixing until thick and lemon colored, about 3 minutes (or whisk by hand for about 5 minutes). Drizzle in the vegetable oil slowly. (If making by hand, whisk constantly as you add the oil. The idea here is for the egg mixture to slowly absorb the oil to make an emulsion. If the oil separates from the mixture, you are adding it too quickly. It should take you at least 3 minutes to add the oil.) Reduce the mixer speed

to low. Add the flour mixture in thirds, mixing until smooth and scraping down the sides of the bowl as needed. Using a rubber spatula, fold in the carrots and walnuts. Divide the batter equally between the prepared pans and smooth the tops.

3. Bake until the cakes are golden brown and a wooden toothpick inserted in the center comes out clean, 40 to 45 minutes. Let cool in the pans on wire cooling racks for 10 minutes. Invert and unmold onto the racks and peel off the paper. Turn the cakes right-side up and let cool completely.

4. Using a long serrated knife, trim the tops of the cake layers so they are flat and even. Place one cake layer on a 7-in/17-cm cardboard cake round. Spread the layer with about 1 cup/230 g of the frosting. Top with the second cake layer, trimmed-side down. Transfer the cake to a decorating turntable. Frost the top, and then the sides, with the remaining frosting. (The sides will be

covered with walnuts, so don't worry if the frosting is thin in that area.) Working on a rimmed baking sheet, press the walnuts onto the sides and top of the cake, letting the excess fall onto the baking sheet and reapplying until the cake is covered. If you like, decorate the top of the cake with frosting carrots. Refrigerate for at least 1 hour (or up to 2 days) before serving.

FROSTING CARROTS

At the bakery, we decorate our carrot cake with carrots made from frosting. Here's how to do it: Put 8 Tbsp/115 g of white frosting in a small bowl and tint with orange food coloring paste or gel. (It is better and easier to buy orange coloring, rather than mix red and yellow to get the right hue.) Add the coloring judiciously, as it is easy to make the frosting too bright. Put 4 Tbsp/60 g of white frosting in a second small bowl and tint with leaf-green food coloring paste or gel.

Transfer the orange frosting to a pastry bag fitted with a $\frac{1}{8}$-in/3-mm plain writing tip, such as Wilton number 6. Pipe one or two practice carrots onto a piece of wax paper: Holding the tip about $\frac{1}{2}$ in/12 mm from the wax paper, squeeze the frosting into an elongated, carrot-shaped squiggle with a pointed end. Scrape your practice carrot(s) back into the orange frosting bowl. Spacing them evenly apart, starting about 1 in/2.5 cm from the edge of the cake, pipe ten or twelve carrots, each about 1 in/2.5 cm long, around the perimeter of the top of the cake. Discard the remaining orange frosting. Wash, dry, and cool the pastry bag and tip. (If the bag and tip are hot, the frosting will melt.) Refill the bag with the green frosting. Now pipe a few green lines on top of each carrot to represent the greens. When you cut the cake, cut the slices on either side of each carrot, so the top of each wedge sports one.

COCONUT CAKE

MAKES 10 TO 12 SERVINGS

This all-American cake is a perennial favorite at the bakery. We make ours with coconut inside and out—in the batter and over the icing. If you are not overly fond of very sweet "boiled" icing (it is only the syrup that is boiled, and not the icing itself), frost the cake with either Vanilla Buttercream (page 134) or Cream Cheese Frosting (page 136).

1 cup/225 g unsalted butter, at room temperature, plus more for the pans

Unbleached all-purpose flour for the pans

3 cups/390 g cake flour (not self-rising)

2 tsp baking powder

¾ tsp fine sea salt

2 cups/400 g sugar

3 large eggs, separated, plus 2 large egg whites, at room temperature

2 tsp pure vanilla extract

1 cup/240 ml canned coconut milk, shaken well before measuring

3 cups/210 g sweetened shredded coconut

1 recipe Old-Fashioned Boiled Icing (page 137)

1. Position a rack in the center of the oven and preheat to 350°F/180°C/gas 4. Lightly butter three 8-in/20-cm round cake pans that have 2-in/5-cm sides. Line the bottoms with parchment or wax paper rounds. Dust the insides of the pans with all-purpose flour and tap out the excess.

2. Sift the cake flour, baking powder, and salt together into a medium bowl. Beat the butter in a large bowl with an electric mixer set on medium-high speed until the butter is smooth, about 1 minute (or by hand with a wooden spoon). Gradually beat in the sugar and mix, scraping down the sides of the bowl often, until light in color and texture, about 4 minutes (or about 10 minutes by hand). One at a time, add the egg yolks, beating well after each addition. Beat in the vanilla. Reduce the mixer speed to low. Add the flour mixture in thirds, alternating them with two equal additions of the coconut milk, mixing after each addition just until smooth and scraping down the sides of the bowl as needed. Mix in 1⅓ cups/115 g of the shredded coconut.

3. With clean beaters, beat the egg whites in a grease-free medium bowl until soft peaks form. Stir about one-fourth of the

egg whites into the batter to lighten the mixture, and then use a rubber spatula to fold in the remaining whites. Divide the batter evenly among the prepared pans and smooth the tops.

4. Bake until the cakes are golden brown and a wooden toothpick inserted in the center comes out clean, 25 to 30 minutes. Let cool in the pans on wire cooling racks for 10 minutes. Invert and unmold onto the racks and peel off the paper. Turn the cakes right-side up and let cool completely.

5. Using a long serrated knife, trim the tops of the cake layers so they are flat and even. Place one cake layer on a 7-in/17-cm cardboard cake round. Spread with about 1 cup/80 g of the icing. Top with a second cake layer and spread with another 1 cup/80 g of icing. Place the final cake layer, trimmed-side down, on the stacked layers. Frost the top, and then the sides, with the remaining icing. Working on a rimmed baking sheet, press the remaining coconut onto the sides and top of the cake, letting the excess fall onto the baking sheet and reapplying until the cake is covered. The cake can be stored under a cake dome at room temperature for up to 2 days.

THE MODEL BAKERY COOKBOOK

FREEZING BAKED GOODS

It may be difficult to find the time to construct a frosted triple-layer cake in one day. We suggest baking and freezing the cake layers ahead of time, so that step is out of the way. Then, all you have to do is frost the layers the day of serving. Freezing is a time-honored technique used by professional bakers to allow the creation of cakes as they are needed for sale. (Not all frostings freeze well, so it is best just to freeze the un-iced layers.) Here are some tips for freezing baked goods:

CAKE LAYERS Wrap the completely cooled cake layers tightly in plastic wrap, and slip them into plastic freezer storage bags for extra support. Freeze the layers for up to 2 months. Before using, unwrap and thaw at room temperature for about 2 hours before frosting.

INDIVIDUAL PASTRIES Some bakers recommend freezing unbaked pastries, such as Danish, croissants, muffins, and buns. We find that they take up a lot of room in the freezer, and the time needed for thawing and rising becomes a guessing game. It is much more convenient to freeze baked pastries, and to thaw or reheat the individual pastries for a quicker-than-quick breakfast. Loosely pack completely cooled pastries in plastic freezer storage bags and freeze for up to 2 months. Remove them, as needed, from the bag. Bake, unthawed, in a preheated 300°F/150°C/gas 2 oven (a toaster oven is perfect for baking one or two pastries) until heated through and thawed, for 10 to 15 minutes, or let stand at room temperature until thawed, about 1½ hours.

BREADS Unsliced loaves of bread can be cooled, wrapped in a double layer of aluminum foil, and frozen for up to 1 month. Unwrap and thaw for a few hours at room temperature before serving. If you wish, bake the loaf in a preheated 350°F/180°C / gas 4 oven for about 10 minutes to crisp the crust.

PIECRUSTS AND TART SHELLS These can be frozen raw, an enormous help when you need to make a bunch of freshly baked Thanksgiving pies. It is most efficient to roll out the dough and use it to line a freezer-safe (metal) pie pan. Freeze the lined pan, uncovered, for about 30 minutes, or until the dough is firm. Wrap the lined pan in a double thickness of plastic wrap, pressing the first layer of wrap directly onto the surface of the dough. Freeze the lined pans for up to 1 month. (You can stack them on top of each other to save space in the freezer.) The piecrust does not need to be thawed before filling and baking—just add a few extra minutes to the baking time. You can wrap and freeze disks of rolled dough and defrost them overnight in the refrigerator before using, but the lined pans are the real time-savers. Also, freezing piecrust is much better than freezing filled pies because some pies take a long time to thaw. The same technique can be used to freeze tart shells.

RED VELVET CAKE

MAKES 10 TO 12 SERVINGS

When did red velvet cake elbow its way into the forefront of beloved American desserts? Southerners, Canadians, and New Yorkers claim it as their own, all with equal fervor. Our version stands up to any version you may have had. It contains oil, and not butter, as its main fat, which gives it a moist tenderness that other renditions lack. And with the rich cream cheese frosting, you will not miss the butter. You can leave the food coloring out, but the cake will be brown. Knowing how popular these are at kids' parties, we also provide a cupcake variation.

Butter, at room temperature, for the pans

Unbleached all-purpose flour for the pans

3¾ cups/485 g cake flour (not self-rising)

3 Tbsp natural cocoa powder

1½ tsp fine sea salt

1½ cups/360 ml buttermilk

1 Tbsp plus 1 tsp liquid red food coloring

1½ tsp pure vanilla extract

2¼ cups/540 ml vegetable oil

2¼ cups/450 g sugar

3 large eggs, at room temperature

2¼ tsp distilled white vinegar

2¼ tsp baking soda

1 recipe Cream Cheese Frosting (page 136)

1. Position a rack in the center of the oven and preheat to 350°F/180°C/gas 4. Lightly butter three 8-in/20-cm round cake pans that have 2-in/5-cm sides. Line the bottoms with parchment or wax paper rounds. Dust the insides of the pans with all-purpose flour and tap out the excess.

2. Sift the cake flour, cocoa powder, and salt together into a medium bowl. Stir the buttermilk, food coloring, and vanilla together in a glass measuring cup or pitcher. Combine the vegetable oil and sugar in the bowl of a stand mixer. Beat on high speed with the whisk attachment until pale, about 3 minutes (or whisk by hand for about 5 minutes). Reduce the mixer speed to medium. Beat in the eggs, one at a time, beating well after each addition. Reduce the speed to low. Add the flour mixture in thirds, alternating them with two equal additions of the buttermilk mixture, mixing after each addition just until combined and scraping

down the sides of the bowl as needed. (Do not change to the paddle attachment, as the whisk does the best job of incorporating the coloring.) Pour the vinegar into a ramekin or custard cup and stir in the baking soda. Add to the batter and mix until thoroughly incorporated. Divide the batter evenly among the prepared pans (it will be on the thin side and will not need to be spread out).

3. Bake until a wooden toothpick inserted in the center comes out clean, about 30 minutes. Let cool in the pans on wire cooling racks for 10 minutes. Run a knife around the inside of each pan to loosen the cake. Invert and unmold onto the racks and peel off the paper. Turn the cakes right-side up and let cool completely.

4. Using a long serrated knife, trim the tops of the cake layers so they are flat and even. Crumble enough of the cake trimmings to make ½ cup/50 g crumbs. (The remaining cake trimmings are the baker's treat.)

CONTINUED

RED VELVET CAKE
CONTINUED

5. Transfer ½ cup/115 g of the frosting to a pastry bag fitted with a ³/₁₆-in/2-mm plain round tip; set aside for the final decoration. Place one cake layer on a 7-in/17-cm cardboard cake round. Spread with about ⅔ cup/155 g of the frosting. Top with a second cake layer and spread with another ⅔ cup/155 g of frosting. Place the final cake layer, trimmed-side down, on the stacked layers. Transfer the cake to a decorating turntable. Frost the top and sides of the cake with a thin layer of the frosting. Refrigerate until the frosting is set, about 20 minutes. Return to the turntable. Frost with the remaining frosting.

6. Working on a rimmed baking sheet, press the cake crumbs into the frosting around the bottom perimeter of the cake, a handful at a time, making a border about ½ in/12 mm high. (You will have leftover crumbs.) Using the frosting in the pastry bag, and starting in the center of the top of the cake, pipe a spiral over the cake top. Refrigerate for at least 1 hour before serving. (The cake can be refrigerated, loosely covered with plastic wrap, for up to 2 days.) Let stand at room temperature for about 30 minutes before serving.

RED VELVET CUPCAKES: Line twenty-two standard muffin cups with paper liners. Using a number-16 food-portion scoop with about a ¼-cup/60-ml capacity, divide the batter evenly among the lined cups. Bake in a preheated 350°F/180°C/gas 4 oven until a cupcake springs back when pressed in the center with a fingertip, about 20 minutes. Let cool in the pan for 5 minutes. Remove the cupcakes from the pan, transfer to wire cooling racks, and let cool completely. Half fill a pastry bag fitted with a ³/₈-in/1-cm star tip with the frosting. Using your fingers, crumble two of the cupcakes into fine crumbs. Swirl the frosting on top of each cupcake, refilling the pastry bag as needed, and sprinkle with the crumbs. Makes 20 cupcakes.

AUNTIE EMMA'S BUTTERMILK CAKE

MAKES THREE 8-IN/20-CM CAKE LAYERS

This recipe is from our Auntie Emma, who owned a restaurant in Portland for many years. It was forever impressed upon Karen that a from-scratch cake is always best. In fact, her mother wouldn't allow cake mixes in the house. (Since they were forbidden fruit, they had extra allure, and Karen and her teenage girlfriends would secretly bake cake mixes, tinted in crazy hues with artificial food coloring.) This is the cake that Auntie Emma would always bring to the annual family reunions in Oregon. The Berries and Cream Cake (page 120) was inspired by those memories.

---

1 cup/225 g unsalted butter, at room temperature, plus more for the pans

Unbleached all-purpose flour for the pans

2¾ cups/355 g cake flour (not self-rising)

1 tsp baking powder

1 tsp baking soda

½ tsp fine sea salt

1¼ cups/300 ml buttermilk

1 tsp pure vanilla extract

1¾ cups/350 g sugar

4 large eggs, at room temperature

1. Position a rack in the center of the oven and preheat to 350°F/180°C/gas 4. Lightly butter three 8-in/20-cm round cake pans that have 2-in/5-cm sides. Line the bottoms with parchment or wax paper rounds. Dust the insides of the pans with all-purpose flour and tap out the excess.

2. Sift the cake flour, baking powder, baking soda, and salt together into a medium bowl. Stir the buttermilk and vanilla together in a glass measuring cup or small pitcher. Beat the butter in a large bowl with an electric mixer set on medium-high speed (or by hand with a wooden spoon) until the butter is smooth, about 1 minute. Gradually beat in the sugar and mix, scraping down the sides of the bowl often, until very pale in color and light in texture, about 4 minutes (or about 10 minutes by hand). Beat in the eggs, one at a time, beating until absorbed after each addition. Reduce the mixer speed to low. Add the flour mixture in thirds, alternating them with two equal additions of the buttermilk mixture, mixing after each addition just until smooth and scraping down the sides of the bowl as needed. Divide the batter evenly among the prepared pans and smooth the tops. Rap the cake pans on the work surface to disperse any air bubbles.

3. Bake until the cakes are golden brown and a wooden toothpick inserted in the center comes out clean, about 30 minutes. Let cool in the pans on wire cooling racks for 10 minutes. Invert and unmold onto the racks and peel off the paper. Turn the cakes right-side up and let cool completely. The cakes can be stored, wrapped in plastic wrap, at room temperature for up to 1 day.

DEVIL'S FOOD CAKE

MAKES THREE 8-IN/20-CM CAKE LAYERS

You'll make this your go-to chocolate cake, just as we have; it's in the Chocolate Mousse Cake (page 124) and Chocolate–Raspberry Cake (page 122). You might be surprised to see brewed coffee providing the batter's liquid, but coffee and chocolate are old friends and enhance each other's flavor. Be sure the brewed coffee is full-flavored and completely cooled to room temperature. (On a personal note, John and Karen had a chocolate cake for their wedding, which was quite scandalous at the time. Sarah and Chris followed suit.)

¾ cup/170 g unsalted butter, at room temperature, plus more for the pans

Unbleached all-purpose flour for the pans

2¼ cups/295 g cake flour (not self-rising)

¾ cup/75 g Dutch-processed cocoa powder

1½ tsp baking soda

¾ tsp fine sea salt

½ tsp baking powder

2¼ cups/450 g sugar

3 large eggs, at room temperature

1½ cups/360 ml brewed coffee, at room temperature

1. Position a rack in the center of the oven and preheat to 350°F/180°C/gas 4. Lightly butter three 8-in/20-cm round cake pans that have 2-in/5-cm sides. Line the bottoms with parchment or wax paper rounds. Dust the insides of the pans with all-purpose flour and tap out the excess.

2. Sift the cake flour, cocoa powder, baking soda, salt, and baking powder together into a medium bowl. Beat the butter in a large bowl with an electric mixer set on medium-high speed (or by hand with a wooden spoon) until the butter is smooth, about 1 minute. Gradually beat in the sugar and mix, scraping down the sides of the bowl often, until very pale in color and light in texture, about 4 minutes (or about 10 minutes by hand). Beat in the eggs, one at a time, beating until absorbed after each

addition. Reduce the mixer speed to low. Add the flour mixture in thirds, alternating them with two equal additions of the coffee, mixing after each addition just until smooth and scraping down the sides of the bowl as needed. Divide the batter evenly among the prepared pans and smooth the tops. Rap the cake pans on the work surface to disperse any air bubbles.

3. Bake until the cakes spring back when gently pressed with a fingertip and a wooden toothpick inserted in the center comes out clean, about 25 minutes. Let cool in the pans on wire cooling racks for 10 minutes. Invert and unmold onto the racks and peel off the paper. Turn the cakes right-side up and let cool completely. The cakes can be stored, wrapped in plastic wrap, at room temperature for up to 1 day.

WHITE CAKE

MAKES THREE 9-IN/23-CM CAKE LAYERS

There are many things to love about this yolkless cake. Brides often prefer it for wedding cakes because the crumb is the traditional white color. This is a moist, delicate cake for any occasion.

---

1 cup/225 g unsalted butter, at room temperature, plus more for the pans

Unbleached all-purpose flour for the pans

4 cups/520 g cake flour (not self-rising)

1 Tbsp plus 1 tsp baking powder

¾ tsp fine sea salt

1⅓ cups/315 ml whole milk

2 tsp pure vanilla extract

2 cups/400 g sugar

8 large egg whites, at room temperature

1. Position a rack in the center of the oven and preheat to 350°F/180°C/gas 4. Lightly butter three 8-in/20-cm round cake pans that have 2-in/5-cm sides. Line the bottoms with parchment or wax paper rounds. Dust the insides of the pans with all-purpose flour and tap out the excess.

2. Sift the cake flour, baking powder, and salt together into a medium bowl. Stir the milk and vanilla together in a glass measuring cup. Beat the butter in a large bowl with an electric mixer set on medium-high speed (or by hand with a wooden spoon) until the butter is smooth, about 1 minute. Gradually beat in the sugar and mix, scraping down the sides of the bowl often, until very pale in color and light in texture, about 4 minutes (or about 10 minutes by hand). Reduce the mixer speed to low. Add the flour mixture in thirds, alternating them with two equal additions of the milk mixture, mixing after each addition just until smooth and scraping down the sides of the bowl as needed.

3. With clean beaters, beat the egg whites in a grease-free medium bowl until soft peaks form. Stir about one-fourth of the egg whites into the batter to lighten the mixture, and then use a rubber spatula to fold in the remaining egg whites. Divide the batter evenly among the prepared pans and smooth the tops.

4. Bake until the cakes are golden brown and a wooden toothpick inserted in the center comes out clean, about 25 minutes. Let cool in the pans on wire cooling racks for 10 minutes. Invert and unmold onto the racks and peel off the paper. Turn the cakes right-side up and let cool completely. The cakes can be stored, wrapped in plastic wrap, at room temperature for up to 1 day.

SUNNY LEMON CAKE

MAKES 10 TO 12 SERVINGS

Driving through the Valley in the winter, you will see countless lemon trees bearing their bright yellow fruit. We are fortunate to have many friends with overloaded trees who are happy to trade for a warm baguette! Our Sunny Lemon Cake is a little tart, a little sweet, and entirely delicious.

LEMON MOUSSE FILLING

½ cup/120 ml heavy cream

1 Tbsp sugar

½ cup/120 ml Lemon Curd (page 162)

½ cup/120 ml Simple Syrup (page 127)

2 Tbsp fresh lemon juice

1 recipe White Cake (facing page)

1 recipe Lemon Buttercream (see page 135)

½ cup plus 2 Tbsp/150 ml Lemon Curd (page 162)

1. **TO MAKE THE FILLING:** Whip the cream and sugar together in a chilled medium bowl with an electric mixer set on high speed until stiff. Fold in the lemon curd.

2. Mix the simple syrup and lemon juice together in a small bowl. Using a long serrated knife, trim the tops of the cake layers so they are flat and even. Place one cake layer on a 7-in/17-cm cardboard cake round. Brush with one-third of the syrup mixture.

3. Transfer about 1½ cups/300 g of the buttercream to a pastry bag fitted with a ⅜-in/1-cm star tip. Pipe a thick line of buttercream around the perimeter of the cake layer. This creates a dam to contain the lemon mousse filling. Spread the area inside the buttercream dam with half of the filling, making sure the filling reaches the edge of the dam. Refrigerate the cake layer for about 20 minutes to firm the filling.

4. Top with another cake layer and brush with half of the remaining syrup. Pipe a buttercream dam around the perimeter of the top cake layer and spread the area inside with the remaining filling. Refrigerate the layers for another 20 minutes. Top with the final cake layer, trimmed-side down, and brush with the remaining syrup.

5. Frost the top, and then the sides, of the cake with a thin layer of buttercream. Refrigerate until the frosting is set, about 20 minutes. Frost with the remaining buttercream, giving it a smooth finish. Transfer the cake to a decorating turntable. Holding the teeth of a decorating comb against the frosting on the side of the cake, rotate the cake to create decorative ridges on the frosting. Spread the lemon curd on top of the cake, leaving a ½-in/12-mm border around the perimeter. Using the buttercream in the bag, pipe a scalloped border around the lemon curd (see Note). Refrigerate until ready to serve, up to 1 day. Let stand at room temperature for 30 minutes before serving.

NOTE: *To pipe a scalloped border, hold the pastry tip just above the top of the cake and pipe a small mound of buttercream on the cake. Without lifting the tip, draw it toward you, slightly relieving the pressure on the bag, to form a scallop about ½ in/12 mm long. Without lifting the tip, pipe another scallop, and repeat around the edge of the cake to make a continuous border. You can also look online for a video; search for "scalloped border cake decorating video."*

BERRIES AND CREAM CAKE

MAKES 10 TO 12 SERVINGS

Of all the cakes we make, this one gives the home baker the most leeway for creative expression. Here is the recipe for its most basic incarnation, with strawberries, but you can use any berries that are in season. For the cake, choose either buttermilk or white cake; they are equally good. (However, my Auntie Emma always used the buttermilk for her famous strawberry cream cake, which was this cake's inspiration.)

FILLING

1 qt/455 g fresh strawberries, raspberries, blueberries, blackberries, or a combination

1 cup/240 ml heavy cream

1 Tbsp sugar

1 recipe White Cake (page 118) or Auntie Emma's Buttermilk Cake (page 116)

½ cup/120 ml Simple Syrup (page 127)

1 recipe Vanilla Buttercream (page 134)

APRICOT GLAZE

⅓ cup/100 g apricot jam or preserves

1 Tbsp water

1. **TO MAKE THE FILLING:** Reserve 5 or 6 of the best-looking berries for a garnish. Hull the remaining strawberries and cut into ¼-in/6-mm dice. Spread out the diced berries on paper towels to drain while you're whipping the cream.

2. Whip the cream and sugar together in a chilled medium bowl with an electric mixer set on high speed until stiff. Fold in the berries.

3. Using a long serrated knife, trim the tops of the cake layers so they are flat and even. Place one cake layer on a 7-in/17-cm cardboard cake round. Brush with one-third of the simple syrup. Spread with half of the cream mixture. Top with another cake layer, brush with half of the remaining syrup, and spread with the remaining cream mixture. Top with the final cake layer, trimmed-side down, and brush with the remaining syrup. Transfer ½ cup/100 g of the buttercream to a pastry bag fitted with a ⅜-in/1-cm plain round tip; set aside at room temperature.

4. Transfer the cake to a decorating stand. Frost the top, and then the sides, of the cake with a thin layer of buttercream.

Refrigerate until the buttercream is set, about 30 minutes. Return the cake to the turntable and frost with the remaining buttercream in the bowl, giving it a smooth finish. Holding the teeth of a decorating comb against the frosting on the side of the cake, rotate the cake to create decorative ridges on the frosting. Refrigerate for at least 1 hour or up to 1 day.

5. **TO MAKE THE GLAZE:** Bring the jam and water to a brisk simmer in a small saucepan over medium heat, stirring often. Cook, stirring often, until thickened, about 1 minute. When you drop some of the glaze from the spoon, the last drops should be very thick and slow to fall. Strain through a wire sieve into a small bowl.

6. Transfer the cake to a cake platter. Arrange the reserved berries on top of the cake, in the center. Brush the berries with the warm apricot glaze; you may not use all of it. With the buttercream in the pastry bag, pipe a scalloped border (see note, page 119) around the top and bottom edges of the cake. Refrigerate until chilled, at least 1 and up to 8 hours. Let stand at room temperature for 30 minutes before serving.

CHOCOLATE-RASPBERRY CAKE

MAKES 12 SERVINGS

This chocolate cake is a far more sophisticated dessert than the Chocolate Mousse Cake (page 124). The latter is more of an American-style buttercream cake, but this one's dark good looks give it a European feel. We admit it is a pricey cake to make, with the piles of chocolate and mounds of raspberries, but it is well worth the cost.

GANACHE

1¼ lb/570 g semisweet chocolate (no more than 55% cacao), finely chopped

2½ cups/600 ml heavy cream

1 Tbsp light corn syrup

1 recipe Devil's Food Cake (page 117)

1½ pints/510 g fresh raspberries

½ cup/120 ml Simple Syrup (page 127)

½ cup/80 g chocolate vermicelli (also called sprinkles; optional)

1. **TO MAKE THE GANACHE:** Put the chocolate in a large heat-proof bowl. Bring the cream to a simmer in a medium saucepan over medium heat, making sure it doesn't boil over. Pour the hot cream over the chocolate and let stand for 3 minutes to soften the chocolate. Add the corn syrup and whisk until smooth. Refrigerate until cool and thick enough to spread, about 1½ hours. (You can also place the bowl in a larger bowl of ice water and let stand, stirring the ganache often with a rubber spatula, just until beginning to set, about 5 minutes.)

2. Using a long serrated knife, trim the tops of the cake layers so they are flat and even. Set aside the twelve most attractive raspberries for the garnish. Transfer about ½ cup/195 g of the ganache to a pastry bag fitted with a ⅜-in/1-cm star tip; set aside at room temperature. Place one cake layer on a 7-in/17-cm cardboard cake round. Brush with one-third of the simple syrup. Spread with about ¾ cup/290 g of the ganache. Arrange half of the raspberries on the ganache, pressing them gently to

adhere. Repeat with another cake layer, half of the remaining syrup, ¾ cup/290 g of the ganache, and the remaining raspberries. Top with the final cake layer, trimmed-side down, and brush with the remaining syrup.

3. Transfer the cake to a decorating turntable. Frost the top, and then the sides, of the cake with a thin layer of the remaining ganache. Refrigerate until the ganache is set, 20 to 30 minutes. Return the cake to the turntable and spread the remaining ganache over the top and sides of the cake, giving it a smooth finish. Using the ganache in the pastry bag, pipe twelve 1-in-/2.5-cm-tall mounds of ganache around the perimeter of the cake, spacing them about ½ in/12 mm apart. Insert the reserved raspberries between the mounds. Working on a rimmed baking sheet, press handfuls of the chocolate vermicelli on the sides of the cake, if desired. Refrigerate until chilled, at least 1 hour or up to 1 day. Slice, using a sharp, thin knife dipped into hot water before cutting.

CHOCOLATE MOUSSE CAKE

MAKES 10 TO 12 SERVINGS

This is a popular birthday cake for chocolate lovers because it is chocolate through and through, with chocolate cake, chocolate mousse filling, and chocolate buttercream.

CHOCOLATE MOUSSE

4 oz/115 g semisweet chocolate (no more than 55% cacao), finely chopped

1½ cups/360 ml heavy cream

1 tsp light corn syrup

2 Tbsp sugar

1 recipe Devil's Food Cake (page 117)

½ cup/120 ml Simple Syrup (page 127)

1 recipe Chocolate Buttercream (see page 135)

Cocoa powder for decoration

1. **TO MAKE THE MOUSSE:** Put the chocolate in a heat-proof medium bowl. Bring ½ cup/120 ml of the cream to a simmer in a medium saucepan over medium heat, making sure it doesn't boil over. Pour the hot cream over the chocolate and let stand for 3 minutes to soften the chocolate. Add the corn syrup and whisk until smooth. Let stand until cool but not firm, about 30 minutes.

2. Whip the remaining 1 cup/240 ml cream with the sugar in a chilled medium bowl with an electric mixer set on high speed until soft peaks form. Stir about one-quarter of the whipped cream into the chocolate mixture to loosen it, then fold in the remaining cream.

3. Using a long, serrated knife, trim the tops of the cake layers so they are flat and even. Place one cake layer on a 7-in/17-cm cardboard cake round. Brush with one-third of the simple syrup. Transfer about 1 cup/200 g of the buttercream to a pastry bag fitted with a ⁷⁄₁₆-in/1-cm plain tip. Pipe a double-thick line of buttercream around the perimeter of the cake layer. This creates a dam to contain the chocolate mousse filling. Spread the area inside the buttercream dam with half of the mousse, making sure the mousse reaches the edge of the dam. Refrigerate the cake layer for about 20 minutes to firm the buttercream. Top with another cake layer and brush with half of the remaining syrup. Pipe a buttercream dam around the perimeter of the top cake layer and spread the area inside with the remaining mousse. Refrigerate the layers for another 20 minutes. (You may not use all of the mousse.) Top with the final cake layer, trimmed-side down, and brush with the remaining syrup.

4. Return any buttercream in the pastry bag to the remaining buttercream. Transfer the cake to a decorating turntable. Frost the top, and then the sides, of the cake with a thin layer of buttercream. Refrigerate, uncovered, until the buttercream is very firm. Repeat with the remaining buttercream to give the cake a smooth finish, and refrigerate again until firm. Sift a thin dusting of cocoa powder over the top of the cake. Refrigerate until ready to serve, up to 2 days. Let stand at room temperature for 30 minutes before serving.

BÛCHE DE NOËL

MAKES 12 SERVINGS

We can't keep enough of this classic French Christmas dessert in stock during the holidays. Decorated to resemble a Yule log, it looks appropriately woodsy when served on a bed of fresh pine branches and further garnished with edible meringue mushrooms. This recipe makes a good-size cake, suitable for large holiday gatherings, so have a long serving platter ready. You can make the mushrooms several days in advance and the bûche the day before you serve.

Butter, at room temperature, for the pan

CHOCOLATE ROULADE

⅓ cup/45 g cake flour (not self-rising)

⅓ cup/35 g Dutch-process cocoa powder

7 large eggs, at room temperature

½ cup/100 g sugar

1 tsp pure vanilla extract

CHOCOLATE MOUSSE

4 oz/115 g semisweet chocolate (no more than 55% cacao), finely chopped

1½ cups/360 ml heavy cream

1 tsp light corn syrup

2 Tbsp sugar

ESPRESSO SYRUP

¼ cup/60 ml Simple Syrup (page 127)

2 Tbsp brewed espresso (or 1 teaspoon instant espresso dissolved in 2 Tbsp boiling water)

GANACHE

8 oz/225 g semisweet chocolate (no more than 55% cacao), finely chopped

1 cup/240 ml heavy cream

2 tsp light corn syrup

Fresh pine branches for serving (optional)

12 Meringue Mushrooms (page 196)

Sugared Cranberries (page 127), for garnish

Confectioners' sugar for dusting

1. Position a rack in the center of the oven and preheat to 350°F/180°C/gas 4. Lightly butter a half-sheet pan. Line the pan with parchment paper.

2. **TO MAKE THE CHOCOLATE ROULADE:** Sift the flour and cocoa together into a small bowl. Beat the eggs and sugar together in a large bowl with an electric mixer set on high speed until the mixture is pale, triples in volume, and forms a thick ribbon that falls back on itself when the beaters are lifted above the mixture's surface, about 5 minutes. Beat in the vanilla. Sift in the cocoa mixture and fold in with a large rubber spatula until combined but fluffy. Spread out evenly in the lined pan.

3. Bake until the cake springs back when pressed with a fingertip, about 15 minutes. Let cool in the pan for 5 minutes. Run a dinner knife around the inside of the pan

to release the cake. Place a clean kitchen towel over the cake. Top with a large cutting board. Invert the pan with the board and remove the pan to unmold the cake. Carefully peel off the paper. Let the cake cool for 5 minutes. Place a fresh piece of parchment paper on top of the cake. Starting at a long side, roll the cake up in the towel and let stand until ready to use.

4. **TO MAKE THE MOUSSE:** Put the chocolate in a heat-proof medium bowl. Bring ½ cup/120 ml of the cream to a simmer in a medium saucepan over medium heat, making sure it doesn't boil over. Pour the hot cream over the chocolate and let stand for 3 minutes to soften the chocolate. Add the corn syrup and whisk until smooth. Let stand until cool but not firm, about 30 minutes.

5. Whip the remaining 1 cup/240 ml cream with the sugar in a chilled medium bowl with an electric mixer set on high speed until soft peaks form. Stir about one-quarter of the whipped cream into the chocolate mixture to loosen it, then fold in the remaining cream.

CONTINUED

CAKES

6. **TO MAKE THE ESPRESSO SYRUP:** Mix the simple syrup and espresso together in a small bowl.

7. Unroll the cake and discard the paper. Leaving the cake on the towel, brush with the espresso syrup. Spread evenly with the chocolate mousse. Starting at the long side nearest you, roll the cake up, using the towel as an aid. Transfer to a long platter, seam-side down. Cover loosely with plastic wrap and refrigerate until the mousse is chilled and set, about 1 hour.

8. **TO MAKE THE GANACHE:** Put the chocolate in a heat-proof medium bowl. Bring the cream to a simmer in a medium saucepan over medium heat, making sure it doesn't boil over. Pour the hot cream over the chocolate and let stand for 3 minutes to soften the chocolate. Add the corn syrup and whisk until smooth. Let stand until tepid and pourable, about 15 minutes.

9. Trim the ends from the roulade. About 4 in/10 cm from one end of the roulade, cut off a piece on the diagonal; this will become the stump on the bûche. Lay the roulade on a large wire cooling rack set over a half-sheet pan. Place the stump next to the log with the diagonally cut side sitting on the rack. Pour about half of the ganache over the roulade and stump and smooth it with a flexible metal spatula, letting the excess drip down the sides and onto the half-sheet pan. Repeat the procedure so the roulade and stump are completely glazed. Let stand for 5 minutes. Using the spatula, transfer the stump to the top of the roulade to make the bûche. Drag the tines of a fork along the ganache to simulate tree bark. Let stand until the ganache is set but not firm, about 20 minutes. Using a long metal spatula, transfer the bûche to the platter. Refrigerate until chilled, at least 1 hour or up to 1 day.

10. When ready to serve, tuck pine branches under the roulade, if desired. Decorate the platter with meringue mushrooms and sugared cranberries. Dust with confectioners' sugar. To serve, slice the chilled bûche with a long, thin knife dipped into hot water.

SIMPLE SYRUP

MAKES ABOUT ¾ CUP/180 ML

Nothing more than sugar and water boiled together into a light syrup, this sweet liquid is brushed onto cake layers to prevent them from drying out and provide extra flavor. Cakes with butter-based batters harden when refrigerated, and the syrup moistens them so they can be served chilled. You will only use 2 to 3 Tbsp for a cake, but make the entire batch and use it to sweeten iced tea or coffee. You won't have to be concerned about undissolved sugar crystals spoiling your drink. We often mix the syrup with lemon juice and water to make refreshing lemonade in the summer.

½ cup/100 g sugar
½ cup/120 ml water

Bring the sugar and water to a boil in a small saucepan over high heat, stirring constantly. Boil, without stirring, until slightly reduced, about 1 minute. Let cool completely. Transfer to a covered container and store in the refrigerator for up to 1 month.

SUGARED CRANBERRIES

MAKES ½ CUP/50 G

These sparkling little red berry globes are a lovely finish to winter desserts. But in spite of the sugar, they are still quite tart, so they are more of a garnish than a confection.

½ cup/50 g fresh cranberries
¼ cup/50 g sugar
1 Tbsp pasteurized egg whites (available in the refrigerated case at the supermarket)

Line a half-sheet pan with parchment paper. Put the cranberries in a small bowl. Put the sugar in another small bowl. In a third small bowl, whisk the pasteurized egg whites until foamy. Pour over the cranberries and toss well until very thinly coated. A few at a time, letting the excess egg white drip off, put the cranberries in the sugar, toss to coat, and transfer to the lined pan. Let stand until completely dry, at least 2 hours or preferably overnight.

A HOMEMADE WEDDING CAKE

MAKES 24 SERVINGS, PLUS 8 CUPCAKES

Model Bakery is ingrained into the Napa Valley life, and it is our role to provide wedding cakes for the community. Couples come to us for classically simple cakes, such as this one with pearl borders and Swiss dots on the sides. We prefer to decorate the layers with fresh flowers, and besides, hardly anyone uses bridal statuettes any more. Here is a modestly sized wedding cake based on our Berries and Cream Cake (page 120) that can be made at home. Read "Wedding Cakes" on page 133 before you get started.

Butter, at room temperature, for the pans

Unbleached all-purpose flour for the pans

2 recipes Auntie Emma's Buttermilk Cake batter (see page 116)

FILLING
2 lb/910 g fresh strawberries

1 qt/960 ml heavy cream

¼ cup/30 g confectioners' sugar

2 recipes Simple Syrup (page 127)

2 recipes Vanilla Buttercream (page 134)

Edible, nonsprayed flowers, for garnish

1. Position racks in the top third and center of the oven and preheat to 350°F/180°C/gas 4. Lightly butter three 8-in/20-cm round cake pans that have 2-in/5-cm sides. Line the bottoms with parchment or wax paper rounds. Dust the insides of the pans with all-purpose flour and tap out the excess.

2. Divide 1 recipe of the batter evenly among the prepared pans, filling them about one-third full, and smooth the tops. Rap the pans on the work surface to disperse any air bubbles.

3. Bake until the cakes are golden brown and a wooden toothpick inserted in the center comes out clean, about 25 minutes. Let cool in the pans on wire cooling racks for 10 minutes. Invert and unmold onto the racks and peel off the paper. Turn the cakes right-side up and let cool completely.

4. Lightly butter three 6-in/15-cm round cake pans that have 2-in/5-cm sides. Line the bottoms with parchment or wax paper rounds. Dust the insides of the pans with all-purpose flour and tap out the excess.

Line eight standard muffin cups with paper liners.

5. Using the second recipe of batter, pour enough batter into each prepared pan to come one-third up the sides (you will not use all of the batter) and smooth the tops. Using a number-16 food-portion scoop with about a ¼-cup/60-ml capacity, transfer the remaining batter to the muffin cups. Rap the pans on the work surface to disperse any air bubbles.

6. Bake the cakes on the center rack and the cupcakes on the top rack until a wooden toothpick inserted in the center of the cakes and cupcakes comes out clean, 20 to 25 minutes. Let cool in the pans on wire cooling racks for 10 minutes. Invert and unmold the cake layers onto the racks and peel off the paper. Turn the cakes right-side up. Remove the cupcakes from the pans, transfer to cooling racks, and let the cakes and cupcakes cool completely. (The cake and cupcakes can be wrapped in plastic wrap and frozen in plastic ziplock bags for up to 2 months. Thaw completely at room temperature for 2 hours before frosting.)

CONTINUED

7. **TO MAKE THE FILLING:** Freeze the bowl of a heavy-duty stand mixer in the freezer to chill. (If the bowl won't fit into your freezer, fill the bowl with ice cubes to chill it for about 10 minutes. Discard the ice and dry the bowl.)

8. Hull the berries and cut into ¼-in/6-mm dice. Spread the berries on paper towels and let drain while whipping the cream. Pour the cream and confectioners' sugar into the chilled mixer bowl. Affix the bowl to the mixer and fit with the whisk attachment. Whip on low speed until the mixture begins to thicken. Increase the speed to medium and whip until the cream is stiff. Fold in the chopped strawberries.

9. Using a long serrated knife, trim the tops of all the cake layers so they are flat and even. Stack the larger layers into a triple-layer tier, and repeat with the smaller layers. Place side by side to check that they are the same height, and trim the top layers as needed.

10. Place one 8-in/20-cm cake layer on a 7-in/17-cm cardboard cake round. Brush with about 1½ Tbsp of the simple syrup. Spread with about 3 cups/600 g of the filling. Top with another cake layer, brush with another 1½ Tbsp syrup, and spread with 3 cups/600 g filling. Top with the final cake layer, trimmed-side down, and brush with 1½ Tbsp syrup. Loosely cover the stacked layers with plastic wrap and refrigerate for 20 minutes to firm the filling.

11. Place one 6-in/15-cm cake layer on a 5 in/12 cm cardboard cake round. Repeat the process, using about 1 Tbsp simple syrup and 1¾ cups/350 g filling on each layer. Loosely cover the stacked cakes and refrigerate for 20 minutes. Tightly cover the remaining filling and refrigerate.

12. Measure 1 cup/200 g of the buttercream into a small bowl, cover, and refrigerate for the final decoration. Transfer the larger cake tier to a decorating turntable. Frost the top, and then the sides, of the cake with a thin layer of buttercream, about 1½ cups/300 g. The filling may want to mix into the buttercream, but don't worry, as it will firm up when refrigerated. Refrigerate uncovered to set the buttercream, about 30 minutes.

13. Repeat with the smaller cake tier, using about 1 cup/200 g of the buttercream. Refrigerate for 30 minutes. Add any remaining buttercream to the reserved buttercream in the refrigerator.

14. Return the larger layered cake to the turntable and frost completely and evenly with another layer of the buttercream. Refrigerate again to set, about 15 minutes. Repeat with the smaller layered cake.

15. Spread a large dab of buttercream on the center of a foil-covered baseboard, and center the larger cake layer on the baseboard. Spacing them evenly, insert three wooden cake dowels in a 4-in/10-cm triangle in the center of the cake with a fourth dowel in the center of the triangle

CONTINUED

for extra support. Remove the dowels and cut them with a serrated knife so the tops of the dowels are flush with the top of the frosted cake. Reinsert the dowels in the cake. Center the smaller cake layer on top of the larger cake layer, supported by the dowels.

16. Fit a pastry bag with a $5/16$-in/6-mm round tip and fill the bag with about half of the remaining buttercream. With the frosting in the pastry bag, pipe pearl-size balls around the top and bottom edges of the top and bottom cakes.

17. Return any buttercream from the pastry bag to the bowl of buttercream. Fit the pastry bag with a $3/16$-/2-mm round tip. Half fill the pastry bag with buttercream. Using the tip of a wooden toothpick, mark your desired pattern of Swiss dots. Using the pastry tip, cover the marks with small dots of buttercream.

18. Using the tip of a small sharp knife, cut out and discard a cone from the center of each cupcake. Fill the space in each cupcake with some of the leftover cream filling, and smooth the top. Brush the exposed cake with syrup. Frost each with the remaining buttercream. You may not use all of the buttercream, filling, and syrup.

19. Refrigerate the entire cake on the baseboard and the cupcakes until chilled, at least 2 hours and up to 1 day.

20. One to two hours before serving, remove the cake from the refrigerator. Arrange the flowers in the center of the top layer. If you wish, top each cupcake with small blossoms from the garnishing flowers (such as a rose petal or violet or two). Do not let the cake stand at room temperature for longer than 2 hours. Slice the cake and serve with the cupcakes.

WEDDING CAKES

Aesthetics aside, the most important thing to keep in mind when making a tiered cake is space. Clear out your kitchen refrigerator so you have room to chill the frosted layers. You will need a separate shelf for each stacked cake. If you have an auxiliary refrigerator in your garage or basement, utilize it to store the cake, or enlist a neighbor's fridge. (Unless your circumstances are very unusual, this means that most of your home's refrigeration will be used to hold the cake, and you will not have room for other food. This is crucial if you are catering other courses of the meal, too.) Keep the cake chilled for as long as possible before setting it up and, if serving outside, be sure that the cake's display area is in a shaded spot.

You will have the best experience as a wedding-cake maker if the components are prepared in stages. Bake, cool, wrap, and freeze the layers up to 2 months ahead. Make and refrigerate the syrup and buttercream a few days ahead; let the frosting come to room temperature before using. Gather all of your equipment and clear a large area in the kitchen for the project.

Rather than worrying about having the exact amount of batter for the cake layers, make a double batch and use any leftover batter to bake cupcakes. Serve the cupcakes to the kids or guests who don't want a standard portion.

Surprisingly, this masterpiece requires very few special items, all available at craft shops and online. Have three 8-in/20-cm cake pans and three 6-in/15-cm cake pans (all 2 in/5 cm deep), and a standard muffin pan and paper liners for the cupcakes. Wooden dowels for cakes, available at craft shops, will help stabilize the stacked layers. These rods are 12 in/30.5 cm long and about ¼ in/6 mm in diameter, and made from soft wood that is easy to cut to size with a serrated knife. You can also use oversize plastic straws, and snip them to size with scissors. Only two plain round pastry tips, ³⁄₁₆ in/2 mm and ⁵⁄₁₆ in/6 mm, are used for the buttercream decorations. Be sure you have enough wire cooling racks for the six layers and cupcakes. You will want a large foil-covered composite cake baseboard for holding the finished cake, and standard 9-in/23-cm cardboard cake rounds (they can be cut to size) for the layers.

Choose some edible, nonsprayed flowers for the crowning touch (we are partial to baby roses from our garden). And don't forget to pour yourself a glass of bubbly to celebrate your job well done.

VANILLA BUTTERCREAM

MAKES ABOUT 4 CUPS/820 G,
ENOUGH TO FROST THREE 8-IN/20-CM OR TWO 9-IN/23-CM CAKE LAYERS

Many a bakery has lost its reputation on the poor quality of its buttercream frosting—greasy stuff that never came near a stick of butter. We have no such worries here at the Model Bakery, as our buttercream is the real thing. A couple of caveats: First, make sure the cooked meringue base is beaten until it is absolutely cool—this takes at least 5 minutes with a stand mixer and longer with a handheld one. The butter should be at cool room temperature, malleable but not so soft that it becomes shiny. Basic buttercream can be flavored to make many variations, so it is a workhorse.

1¼ cups/250 g sugar

5 large egg whites

2 cups/455 g unsalted butter, at room temperature

1 tsp pure vanilla extract

1. Combine the sugar and egg whites in the bowl of a stand mixer or, to use a handheld mixer, in a large heat-proof bowl, preferably stainless steel. Choose a saucepan that will hold the mixing bowl snugly. Put about 2 in/5 cm water in the saucepan and bring to a simmer over high heat. Reduce the heat to low. Put the bowl in the saucepan over the water—the bottom of the bowl should not touch the water. Whisk constantly by hand, scraping down any splashes of egg white on the sides of the bowl with a heat-proof spatula, until the mixture is hot to the touch and white in color and the sugar is completely dissolved, about 2 minutes. The idea here is to stir and warm the whites while dissolving the sugar, not to whip the mixture.

2. Affix the bowl to the mixer and fit with the whisk attachment. Beat on medium-high speed until the mixture forms stiff, shiny peaks and is completely cool, about 10 minutes. (Or beat with an electric mixer on high speed for at least 12 minutes.)

3. Reduce the mixer speed to medium. Beat in the butter, 1 Tbsp at a time, waiting until each addition is absorbed before adding another. Once all the butter has been added, increase the speed to medium-high and continue beating until very light and fluffy, about 1 minute. Beat in the vanilla. The buttercream can be made up to 1 day ahead, transferred to a covered container, and refrigerated. Bring to room temperature, then beat the mixture until fluffy before using.

CHOCOLATE BUTTERCREAM: Decrease the vanilla to ½ tsp. Melt 5 oz/140 g finely chopped semisweet chocolate in the top part of a double boiler over simmering water. (Or melt in a microwave at 50 percent power in 30-second increments, stirring after each one.) Remove from the heat and let cool until tepid but still fluid. Add to the beaten buttercream and mix well. Makes about 4 cups/960 ml.

LEMON BUTTERCREAM: Omit the vanilla. Mix 3 Tbsp Lemon Curd (page 162) into the buttercream. Add a drop of yellow food coloring paste or gel to heighten the color, if you wish.

MOCHA BUTTERCREAM: Decrease the vanilla to ½ tsp. Melt 2 oz/55 g finely chopped semisweet chocolate in the top part of a double boiler over simmering water. (Or melt in a microwave at 50 percent power in 30-second increments, stirring after each one.) Remove from the heat and let cool until tepid but still fluid. Add to the beaten buttercream and mix well. Mix 2 Tbsp cold brewed espresso (or 2 tsp instant espresso dissolved in 2 Tbsp boiling water and cooled) into the buttercream.

ORANGE BUTTERCREAM: Omit the vanilla. Mix the grated zest of 1 orange into the buttercream.

CREAM CHEESE FROSTING

MAKES 4 CUPS/930 G

This American classic is a rich and creamy addition to just about any layer cake. Be sure that the cream cheese is quite soft before mixing.

1 lb/455 g cream cheese, at room temperature

6 Tbsp/85 g unsalted butter, at room temperature

1 tsp pure vanilla extract

3¼ cup/320 g confectioners' sugar, sifted

Combine the cream cheese, butter, and vanilla in the bowl of a stand mixer. Beat on high speed until combined, about 1 minute. Reduce the speed to low. Gradually mix in the confectioners' sugar. Return the speed to high and beat until light and fluffy, about 3 minutes. The frosting can be made up to 1 day ahead, transferred to a covered container, and refrigerated. Bring to room temperature, then beat the mixture until fluffy before using.

OLD-FASHIONED BOILED ICING

MAKES ABOUT 5 CUPS/400 G

Also known as seven-minute icing (because it is beaten for that length of time), this cake coating has an irresistible, marshmallow-like fluffiness. Strangely enough, this icing is not actually boiled.

1½ cups/300 g sugar

½ cup/120 ml water

¼ tsp cream of tartar

4 large egg whites

Pinch of fine sea salt

1 tsp pure vanilla extract

1. Combine the sugar, water, and cream of tartar in a heavy medium saucepan. Bring to a boil over high heat, stirring constantly just until the sugar dissolves. Attach a candy thermometer to the saucepan. Cook, without stirring, occasionally swirling the saucepan by the handle and washing down the crystals on the inside of the saucepan with a bristle brush dipped in water, until the syrup registers 240°F/115°C (soft-ball stage) on the thermometer. Reduce the heat to low to maintain the temperature.

2. Beat the egg whites and salt in the bowl of a stand mixer fitted with the whisk attachment on high speed just until soft peaks form. With the mixer on high speed, drizzle the hot syrup into the whites (pouring near, but not directly into the whisk, where the syrup will splatter, and not down the sides of the bowl, where it could congeal) and whip until stiff, shiny peaks form. Add the vanilla and continue to beat until tepid, about 7 minutes more. If the icing is too thick, beat in hot water, 1 Tbsp at a time, until spreadable. Use the icing while it is warm.

THE MODEL BAKERY ON CAKES

There is no reason why making a layer cake should be done in a single, long work period. Freeze the baked cakes before frosting to save time on the day you will serve the cake. After baking, cool the cake layers, wrap each one in plastic wrap, and slip into a ziplock freezer bag. Freeze for up to 2 months. Thaw in its wrapping at room temperature for a couple of hours before frosting. All of the buttercreams (pages 134 and 135) and the Cream Cheese Frosting (page 136) can be made a few days ahead and refrigerated. Let them stand at room temperature until warm enough to spread, and beat with an electric mixer to restore the fluffiness, if necessary.

While there are many baked goods that can be mixed by hand, cake batter will be best when made with an electric mixer, as it incorporates lots of air into the butter during the creaming process to ensure the cake has a light texture. You can use either a stand or a handheld mixer.

All of the layer cakes use round cake pans 8 in/20 cm in diameter with 2-in-/5-cm-high sides, made from heavy-gauge aluminum. These professional-quality pans are easily found online.

To be sure that your cake layers will be the same height after baking, use a kitchen scale. Just tare the weight of the cake pans, then distribute the batter evenly among the pans.

Cake layers often have a dome, which must be trimmed off before stacking the layers. Use a long serrated knife, held parallel to the work surface, to slice off the dome where it begins. Discard or nibble the trimmings, as you wish. They can also be crumbled and pressed onto the sides of the cake as a decoration, as we do on the Red Velvet Cake (page 113). Freeze the trimmings from Auntie Emma's Buttermilk Cake (page 116) or White Cake (page 118) in a freezer storage bag to use in the filling for Bear Claws (page 71).

For decoration, simple is best. We don't do buttercream flowers or other time-consuming decorations. You can do a lot with only a couple of pastry tips and disposable plastic pastry bags. See page 27 for our recommended basic pastry tips.

A decorating turntable rotates the cake, for the best accessibility when you're frosting. In a pinch, you can set the cake on a flat plate and put the plate on an inverted bowl with a wide base. A metal offset icing spatula is another icing tool that a professional baker would not be without.

Clear an area in your refrigerator to chill the cake during the various stages of filling and frosting the layers. Each filled layer should be chilled (as directed in the recipe) before adding the next layer. Otherwise, if the filling is soft, the finished cake could be lopsided.

Frosting a cake can be easy, and it is one of those jobs where practice does make perfect. If the cake will have icing decorations (such as a pearl or scallop border), transfer about ½ cup/40 g of the icing to a pastry bag fitted with the appropriate tip. Put a dab of icing on a 7-in/17-cm cardboard cake round and top with a cake layer. The icing will help keep the layer in place. (The round is slightly smaller than the cake layer because it allows you to frost the cake without the cardboard getting in the way.) Spread about 1 cup/80 g of the icing evenly over the top of the first layer. Top with the second layer, and spread another 1 cup/80 g of icing over the top. Finish with the third layer, trimmed-side down (the bottom of the layer will provide a smooth surface for the top of the cake). Spread the top, and then the sides, of the cake with a thin layer of icing. This is called a crumb coat, because it helps set in place the loose crumbs that would otherwise mar the frosting. Refrigerate the cake for about 20 minutes to set the icing, keeping the remaining icing at room temperature. Use the remaining icing to finish frosting the cake. Don't worry if the icing on the sides of the cake is thin, especially if it will be masked with coconut, chopped nuts, cake crumbs, chocolate vermicelli, or other ingredients.

 To write an inscription on a cake, melt chocolate (see page 29), and let it cool until tepid and thick enough to pipe. Transfer to a disposable plastic pastry bag (without a tip, because warm chocolate hardens when it touches metal, and the tip will quickly clog). Snip off the end with scissors to make a ⅛-in-/3-mm-wide opening. It helps to do a test run of the inscription on the cake, so you don't run out of space during the actual piping: Trace the baking pan on paper and sketch the inscription with a pencil to see how large the letters can be and still fit. You can also pipe the inscription on parchment paper, let it harden, and then use an offset spatula to carefully lift and transfer the chocolate writing to the top of the cake.

 Layer cakes should be refrigerated for storage, but the butter in the batter or frosting will harden when chilled, making the cake unpleasantly firm. Always let the cake stand at room temperature for 30 minutes to 1 hour so these components can soften before serving. Cut the cake with a long, sharp knife, dipped into a tall glass of hot water between slices.

PIES AND TARTS

At the bakery, you can tell the time of year by the pies in the display case. We use locally grown fruits whenever possible. The Valley and its surrounding area support an amazing variety of produce, and more often than not, our pie and tart fillings utilize the bounty from nearby farmers. One thing we learned early on: Fruit pies are only as good as the produce inside. You can't fix bland, flavorless fruit with sugar and spice, so always use fruit at its seasonal peak. We specialize in streusel-topped pies, because they have an old-fashioned appeal and are quicker to make in a large quantity than double-crust pies. At the end of the chapter you'll find some tips for your homemade pies and tarts.

APPLE STREUSEL PIE

MAKES 8 SERVINGS

We eagerly await the Gravenstein season because these apples make the best apple pies in the world! While apples are a fall crop in most of the country, around here they appear in July and August. Gravensteins don't store or travel well, but you will find them at farmers' markets on the West Coast during their season. When they are gone, we make our pies with a combination of Granny Smith and McIntosh.

FILLING

8 tart, firm apples, preferably Gravenstein, or 4 Granny Smith and 4 McIntosh apples

1 cup/200 g sugar

3 Tbsp unbleached all-purpose flour

½ tsp ground ginger

¼ tsp ground cinnamon

¼ tsp fine sea salt

Unbleached all-purpose flour for rolling out the dough

1 recipe Pie Dough (page 163)

1 recipe Streusel (facing page)

1. **TO MAKE THE FILLING:** Peel and core the apples. Cut into wedges about ¼ in/ 6 mm thick. Transfer to a large bowl; add the sugar, flour, ginger, cinnamon, and salt; and mix well.

2. On a lightly floured work surface, roll out the dough into a round about 13 in/ 33 cm in diameter and ⅛ in/3 mm thick. You will see flakes of flattened butter and shortening in the dough—which is just what you want. Fit the dough into a 9-in/23-cm pie pan. Trim the overhanging dough so it only extends ½ in/12 mm beyond the rim of the pan; discard the trimmings. Working around the perimeter of the pan, fold the dough under so the fold is flush with the rim of the pan, and flute the dough. Freeze for 15 to 30 minutes.

3. Position a rack in the bottom third of the oven and preheat to 400°F/200°C/gas 6. Line a rimmed baking sheet with parchment paper or aluminum foil to catch the drips from the filling.

4. Heap the apples in the pie shell, arranging them so they are closely packed. The apples will shrink during baking, so don't be alarmed that the mound is high at this point. Press handfuls of the streusel over the filling to cover it completely. Put the pie pan on the lined baking sheet.

5. Bake for 20 minutes. Reduce the oven temperature to 350°F/180°C/gas 4. Continue baking until the streusel and crust are browned and the center of the filling is gently bubbling, about 1¼ hours. If the streusel or crust browns too much before the filling is bubbling, tent the pie with aluminum foil. Transfer the pie to a wire cooling rack and let cool completely, which will take a few hours. Cut into wedges and serve. (The pie can be covered with plastic wrap and refrigerated for up to 1 day.)

STREUSEL

ABOUT 2 CUPS/440 G

---

1 cup/145 g unbleached all-purpose flour

⅓ cup plus 1 Tbsp/85 g granulated sugar

⅓ cup plus 1 Tbsp/85 g light brown sugar

1 tsp ground cinnamon

¼ tsp fine sea salt

¾ cup/170 g unsalted butter, at room temperature

1 tsp pure vanilla extract

Mix the flour, granulated sugar, brown sugar, cinnamon, and salt together in a medium bowl. Add the butter. Using your fingertips, rub in the butter until the mixture is homogenous and crumbly. Work in the vanilla.

PEACH STREUSEL PIE

MAKES 8 SERVINGS

Napa Valley has always been farm country; it's just that grapes are the main crop now. John Williams, at Frog's Leap winery, operates a vineyard, winery, and organic farm on their property. We get our peaches from head gardener Degge Hays, in addition to the ones from Karen's farm. Taste the fruit before settling on the amount of sugar, and add a little lemon juice if the peaches are bland.

FILLING

10 ripe peaches

1 cup/200 g sugar, plus more as needed

½ tsp almond extract

2 Tbsp fresh lemon juice (optional)

¼ cup/30 g cornstarch

Unbleached all-purpose flour for rolling out the dough

1 recipe Pie Dough (page 163)

1 recipe Streusel (page 143)

1. **TO MAKE THE FILLING:** Bring a large pot of water to a boil over high heat. Add the peaches and heat just until the peach skins loosen, about 30 seconds. Using a slotted spoon, transfer the peaches to a bowl of ice water. Drain, peel, and pit the peaches, and cut into ½-in/12-mm wedges. Transfer to a large bowl, add the sugar and almond extract, and mix well. Taste and add more sugar or the lemon juice, as needed. Stir in the cornstarch. Let stand for about 30 minutes so the peaches can give up some of their juices.

2. On a lightly floured work surface, roll out the dough into a round about 13 in/33 cm in diameter and ⅛ in/3 mm thick. You will see flakes of flattened butter and shortening in the dough, which is just what you want. Fit the dough into a 9-in/23-cm pie pan. Trim the overhanging dough so it only extends ½ in/12 mm beyond the rim of the pan; discard the trimmings. Working around the perimeter of the pan, fold the dough under so the fold is flush with the rim of the pan, and flute the dough. Freeze for 15 to 30 minutes.

3. Position a rack in the bottom third of the oven and preheat to 400°F/200°C/gas 6. Line a rimmed baking sheet with parchment paper or aluminum foil to catch the drips from the filling.

4. Spread the filling in the pie shell. Press handfuls of the streusel over the filling to cover it completely. Put the pie pan on the lined baking sheet.

5. Bake for 20 minutes. Reduce the oven temperature to 350°F/180°C/gas 4. Continue baking until the streusel and crust are browned and the center of the filling is gently bubbling, about 1¼ hours. If the streusel or crust browns too much before the filling is bubbling, tent the pie with aluminum foil. Transfer the pie to a wire cooling rack and let cool completely, which will take a few hours. Cut into wedges and serve. (The pie can be covered with plastic wrap and refrigerated for up to 1 day.)

PEACH-BERRY STREUSEL PIE:
Sprinkle 6 oz/170 g blackberries or boysenberries over the peaches in step 4. Proceed as directed.

STRAWBERRY-RHUBARB PIE

MAKES 8 SERVINGS

For some people, rhubarb is a take-it-or-leave-it food, but when they taste our strawberry-rhubarb pie, they become fans. In the past, rhubarb was often called pieplant, because the red stalks were one of the first spring crops, and they were immediately cooked to relieve a diet of winter fruit pies. Local strawberries are abundant at our farmers' markets from early spring through the summer.

FILLING

1 qt/455 g strawberries, hulled and sliced

2 cups/250 g sliced rhubarb

1¼ cups/250 g sugar

¼ cup/35 g unbleached all-purpose flour

Grated zest of 1 orange

Unbleached all-purpose flour for rolling out dough

1 recipe Pie Dough (page 163)

1 recipe Streusel (page 143)

1. **TO MAKE THE FILLING:** Mix the strawberries, rhubarb, sugar, flour, and orange zest in a medium bowl. Let stand for 20 to 30 minutes so the berries can give off some of their juices.

2. On a lightly floured work surface, roll out the dough into a round about 13 in/33 cm in diameter and ⅛ in/3 mm thick. You will see flakes of flattened butter and shortening in the dough, which is just what you want. Fit the dough into a 9-in/23-cm pie pan. Trim the overhanging dough so it only extends ½ in/12 mm beyond the rim of the pan; discard the trimmings. Working around the perimeter of the pan, fold the dough under so the fold is flush with the rim, and flute the dough. Freeze for 15 to 30 minutes.

3. Position a rack in the bottom third of the oven and preheat to 400°F/200°C/gas 6. Line a rimmed baking sheet with parchment paper or aluminum foil to catch the drips from the filling.

4. Spread out the filling in the pie shell. Press handfuls of the streusel over the filling to cover it completely. Put the pie pan on the lined baking sheet.

5. Bake for 20 minutes. Reduce the oven temperature to 350°F/180°C/gas 4. Continue baking until the streusel and crust are browned and the center of the filling is gently bubbling, about 1¼ hours. If the streusel or crust browns too much before the filling is bubbling, tent the pie with aluminum foil. Transfer the pie to a wire cooling rack and let cool completely, which will take a few hours. Cut into wedges and serve. (The pie can be covered with plastic wrap and refrigerated for up to 1 day.)

PECAN PIE

MAKES 8 SERVINGS

We make plenty of pecan pies for our restaurant clientele, as well as for the bakery display case. Our recipe has a touch of bourbon, which seems to bring out the other flavors without tasting boozy. Anyone who loves pecan pie will tell you to always serve it with vanilla ice cream or whipped cream to balance the pie's sweetness.

Unbleached all-purpose flour for rolling out the dough

1 recipe Pie Dough (page 163)

FILLING

1 cup/200 g packed light brown sugar

¾ cup/180 ml light corn syrup

4 large eggs, at room temperature

4 Tbsp/55 g unsalted butter, melted and cooled slightly

2 Tbsp bourbon

¾ tsp pure vanilla extract

½ cup/85 g chocolate chips (optional)

2 cups/230 g coarsely chopped pecans

1. On a lightly floured work surface, roll out the dough into a round about 13 in/ 33 cm in diameter and ⅛ in/3 mm thick. You will see flakes of flattened butter and shortening in the dough, which is just what you want. Fit the dough into a 9-in/23-cm pie pan. Trim the overhanging dough so it only extends ½ in/12 mm beyond the rim; discard the trimmings. Working around the perimeter of the pan, fold the dough under so the fold is flush with the rim of the pan, and flute the dough. Freeze for 15 to 30 minutes.

2. Position a rack in the bottom third of the oven and preheat to 400°F/200°C/gas 6.

3. Place the pie pan on a large rimmed baking sheet. Line the pie shell with aluminum foil and fill with pie weights or dried beans. Bake until the edges of the pie dough look set and are just beginning to color, about 15 minutes. Remove the pie pan from the oven, keeping it on the baking sheet.

Remove the foil and pie weights. Continue baking, pressing down the dough with the back of a fork if it puffs, until barely browned, about 5 minutes. Remove from the oven.

4. **TO MAKE THE FILLING**: Whisk the brown sugar, corn syrup, eggs, butter, bourbon, and vanilla in a medium bowl until well combined. Stir in the chocolate chips (if using). Pour into the pie shell. Sprinkle the pecans evenly over the syrup mixture.

5. Put the pie, still on the baking sheet, in the oven. Reduce the oven temperature to 350°F/180°C/gas 4. Bake until the pie filling is puffed all over, about 50 minutes. Transfer the pie to a wire cooling rack and let cool completely, which will take a few hours. Cut into wedges and serve. (The pie can be covered with plastic wrap and refrigerated for up to 1 day.)

BRANDIED PUMPKIN PIE

MAKES 8 SERVINGS

If you have a bakery, people expect you to sell pumpkin pie at Thanksgiving, and you had better comply. The trick is to make your customers take notice of something that they have eaten many times. Our filling has a splash of brandy, crystallized (not ground) ginger, and just enough sugar. It is the nature of pumpkin pie to contract and crack during cooling, so don't be alarmed if this happens to you. Just cover the crevice with a topping of whipped cream.

Unbleached all-purpose flour for rolling out the dough

1 recipe Pie Dough (page 163)

FILLING

One 15-oz/430-g can solid-pack pumpkin

1 cup/240 ml heavy cream

3 large eggs, at room temperature

½ cup/100 g sugar

2 Tbsp minced crystallized ginger, plus more for garnishing

2 Tbsp brandy

½ tsp ground cinnamon

⅛ tsp ground mace

⅛ tsp ground cloves

⅛ tsp fine sea salt

Whipped Cream (page 161) for serving

1. On a lightly floured work surface, roll out the dough into a round about 13 in/ 33 cm in diameter and ⅛ in/3 mm thick. You will see flakes of flattened butter and shortening in the dough, which is just what you want. Fit the dough into a 9-in/23-cm pie pan. Trim the overhanging dough so it only extends ½ in/12 mm beyond the rim of the pan; discard the trimmings. Working around the perimeter of the pan, fold the dough under so the fold is flush with the rim of the pan, and flute the dough. Freeze for 15 to 30 minutes.

2. Position a rack in the bottom third of the oven and preheat to 400°F/200°C/gas 6.

3. Place the pie pan on a large rimmed baking sheet. Line the pie shell with aluminum foil and fill with pie weights or dried beans. Bake until the edges of the pie dough look set and are just beginning to brown, about 15 minutes. Remove the pie pan from the oven, keeping it on the baking sheet. Remove the foil and pie weights.

4. **TO MAKE THE FILLING**: Combine the pumpkin, cream, eggs, sugar, crystallized ginger, brandy, cinnamon, mace, cloves, and salt in a medium bowl and whisk until smooth and well combined. Pour into the pie shell.

5. Put the pie in the oven. Bake for 10 minutes. Reduce the oven temperature to 350°F/ 180°C/gas 4. Bake until the most of the filling has puffed but the very center looks shiny and hasn't quite set, about 40 minutes. Transfer the pie to a wire cooling rack and let cool completely. Refrigerate until the pie is chilled, at least 2 hours or up to 1 day. Top with a dollop of whipped cream, garnish with crystallized ginger, cut into wedges, and serve.

CHOCOLATE AND CARAMEL TARTLETS
WITH FLEUR DE SEL

MAKES 6 TARTLETS

Many of our customers are regular party givers, and they have discovered that a personal tartlet for each guest is an elegant way to serve dessert. While we have a reputation for serving tasty old-fashioned treats, these small chocolate and caramel tarts, finished with a sprinkle of flaky sea salt (*fleur de sel*), are a nod to contemporary tastes. They will keep in the refrigerator for a couple of days, so you can get them done well before guests arrive. You will probably have leftover caramel, but it is difficult to make it in a smaller batch. You can refrigerate the caramel and use it to stir into hot coffee or tea.

CARAMEL

⅓ cup/65 g sugar

2 Tbsp water

½ tsp light corn syrup

3 Tbsp heavy cream

Unbleached all-purpose flour for rolling out the dough

1 recipe Tart Dough (page 164)

GANACHE

1 cup/240 ml heavy cream

8 oz/225 g bittersweet chocolate (no more than 55% cacao), coarsely chopped

About ½ tsp flaky sea salt or fleur de sel, such as Maldon or *fleur de sel de Guérande*

1. **TO MAKE THE CARAMEL:** Stir the sugar, water, and corn syrup together in a small heavy saucepan over high heat until the sugar dissolves. Stop stirring and boil, occasionally rotating the pan by the handle to swirl the syrup, and washing down any crystals that form on the sides of the pan with a bristle brush dipped in cold water, until the syrup is smoking and the color of an old copper coin, about 3 minutes. Remove from the heat. Add the cream and stir until dissolved. Transfer to a small heat-proof ramekin or bowl and let cool.

2. Position a rack in the center of the oven and preheat to 400°F/200°C/gas 6. Have ready six 5-in/12-cm tartlet pans with removable bottoms.

3. Lightly flour the work surface. Divide the dough into six equal portions. Shape each portion into a flat disk. Working with one portion at a time, roll out the dough into a 7-in/17-cm round about ⅛ in/3 mm thick. Fit into a tartlet pan, making sure the dough fits snugly where the base meets the sides. Trim off the excess dough so the dough is flush with the rim of the pan. Press the dough firmly against the sides. Freeze until the dough is firm, 15 to 30 minutes.

4. Place the tartlet pans on a large rimmed baking sheet. Line each shell with aluminum foil and fill with pie weights or dried beans. Bake until the dough looks set and is beginning to brown, about 12 minutes. Remove the baking sheet from the oven. Remove the foil and pie weights. Pierce each tartlet shell a few times with a fork. Return to the oven and bake until golden brown, about 5 minutes. Transfer to a wire cooling rack and let cool completely.

CONTINUED

5. TO MAKE THE GANACHE: Heat the cream in a small saucepan over medium heat until small bubbles form around the edges. Put the chocolate in a medium heat-proof bowl. Add the hot cream and let stand until the chocolate softens, about 3 minutes. Whisk just until smooth. Set aside until slightly cooled, about 30 minutes.

6. Pour an equal amount of the ganache into each pastry shell. Refrigerate until the ganache is set, about 1 hour.

7. Check the consistency of the caramel; it should flow easily from a spoon. If necessary, warm gently in a bowl of hot water, stirring the caramel until fluid. Spoon a ¼-in-/ 6-mm-wide ribbon of caramel across the top of each tartlet. Sprinkle each ribbon with a generous pinch of the salt. Refrigerate until ready to serve. Just before serving, remove the sides of the tartlet pans.

LEMON BRÛLÉE TART

MAKES 8 SERVINGS

One of the many pleasures of living in the Valley is gardening. Throughout the winter, countless lemon trees peek out from behind backyard fences, and often we have more lemons than we know what to do with. This lemon tart, with a "burnt" topping, is a nice way to use them up. You will need a handheld culinary torch to caramelize the sugar on the topping. (Don't try to broil the tart to melt the sugar—we tried once, and it doesn't work.) In the summer, you can serve the tart with fresh blueberries or raspberries.

Unbleached all-purpose flour for rolling out the dough

1 recipe Tart Dough (page 164)

2 recipes Lemon Curd (page 162)

3 Tbsp sugar

1. Position a rack in the center of the oven and preheat to 400°F/200°C/gas 6.

2. Lightly flour the work surface. Roll out the dough into a 13-in/33-cm round about ⅛ in/3 mm thick. Fit into a 9-in/23-cm tart pan with a removable bottom, making sure the dough fits snugly where the base meets the sides. Trim off the excess dough so the dough is flush with the rim of the pan. Press the dough firmly against the sides. Freeze until the dough is firm, 15 to 30 minutes.

3. Place the pan on a large rimmed baking sheet. Line the dough with aluminum foil and fill with pie weights or dried beans. Bake until the dough looks set and is beginning to brown, about 12 minutes. Remove the baking sheet from the oven. Remove the foil and pie weights. Pierce the tart shell a few times with a fork. Return to the oven and continue baking until crisp and golden brown, about 10 minutes. Transfer to a wire cooling rack and let cool completely.

4. Spread out the lemon curd in the tart shell and sprinkle with the sugar. Using a handheld butane kitchen torch, wave the flame about ½ in/12 mm from the top of the tart to melt and caramelize the sugar. Let cool, then refrigerate until ready to serve, up to 8 hours. Just before serving, remove the sides of the tart pan. Cut into wedges and serve.

FRESH FRUIT TART

MAKES 8 SERVINGS

A classic fruit tart should be brightly colored with a rainbow of fruit—purple blackberries, golden-orange mango, and bright red raspberries or strawberries are an especially nice combination. Don't overfill the shell with pastry cream—there should be equal amounts of cream and fruit.

Unbleached all-purpose flour for rolling out the dough

1 recipe Tart Dough (page 164)

APRICOT GLAZE

⅓ cup/100 g apricot jam or preserves

1 Tbsp water

1¼ cups/325 g Pastry Cream (page 161)

About 4 cups/510 g assorted fresh fruit such as blackberries, blueberries, raspberries, or strawberries; peeled, pitted, and sliced mangoes or peaches; peeled and sliced kiwi; sliced figs and honeydew melon balls

1. Position a rack in the center of the oven and preheat to 400°F/200°C/gas 6.

2. Lightly flour the work surface. Roll out the dough into a 13-in/33-cm round about ⅛ in/3 mm thick. Fit into a 9-in/23-cm tart pan with a removable bottom, making sure the dough fits snugly where the base meets the sides. (If the dough breaks, just press it together in the pan.) Trim off the excess dough so the dough is flush with the rim of the pan. Press the dough firmly against the sides. Freeze until the dough is firm, 15 to 30 minutes.

3. Place the pan on a large rimmed baking sheet. Line the dough with aluminum foil and fill with pie weights or dried beans. Bake until the dough looks set and is beginning to brown, about 12 minutes. Remove the baking sheet from the oven.

Remove the foil and pie weights. Pierce the tart shell a few times with a fork. Return to the oven and bake until crisp and golden brown, about 10 minutes. Transfer to a wire cooling rack and let cool completely.

4. **TO MAKE THE GLAZE:** Bring the jam and water to a brisk simmer in a small saucepan over medium heat, stirring often. Cook, continuing to stir often, until thickened, about 1 minute. When you drop some of the glaze from the spoon, the last drops should be very thick and slow to fall. Strain through a wire sieve into a small bowl.

5. Spread out the pastry cream in the tart shell. Top with an assortment of fruit. Brush the warm apricot glaze over the fruit. Refrigerate until ready to serve, up to 1 day. Just before serving, remove the sides of the pan.

GÂTEAU BASQUE

MAKES 8 SERVINGS

Karen discovered this tartlike pastry during a trip to the French Basque region, where it was served for breakfast at a very charming inn. Although *gâteau* means "cake" in French, this is really more of a double-crust tart filled with pastry cream. The dough can be difficult to roll and may crack; just press the pieces together and keep going. Not the most common dessert on these shores, it is well worth adding to your repertoire. This uses an 8-in/20-cm round cake pan with 2-in/5-cm sides, preferably with a removable bottom, which you can find in cake supply shops and online. A springform pan has 3-in/7.5-cm sides and is too tall, but it will work if you don't mind a slightly rustic look.

ALMOND DOUGH

1½ cups/195 g cake flour (not self-rising), plus more for rolling out the dough

⅓ cup/35 g almond flour (see Note)

1 tsp baking powder

¼ tsp fine sea salt

2 large egg yolks

1 Tbsp golden rum

1 tsp almond extract

1 tsp vanilla extract

½ cup/115 g unsalted butter, at room temperature, plus more for the pan

1 cup/200 g sugar

1 recipe Pastry Cream (page 161)

½ cup/150 g cherry preserves or any tart fruit preserves

1 large egg yolk

1 Tbsp heavy cream or milk

1. **TO MAKE THE DOUGH:** Whisk the cake flour, almond flour, baking powder, and salt together in a medium bowl until combined. Mix the egg yolks, rum, almond extract, and vanilla together in a small bowl. Beat the butter in a medium bowl with an electric mixer set on high speed until smooth, about 1 minute. Gradually beat in the sugar and continue beating until light in color and texture, about 2 minutes more. (Or cream the butter and sugar together in a medium bowl with a wooden spoon until light in color and texture, about 5 minutes.) Beat in the yolk mixture. Reduce the mixer speed to low. Gradually add the flour mixture, mixing just until blended.

2. Divide the dough into two flat disks, one slightly larger than the other. Wrap each in plastic wrap and refrigerate for about 30 minutes. The dough is easiest to work with when it is chilled, but not hard.

3. Position a rack in the center of the oven and preheat to 350°F/180°C/gas 4. Lightly butter an 8-in/20-cm round cake pan that has 2-in/5-cm sides, preferably with a removable bottom.

4. On a lightly floured work surface, roll out the larger disk of dough into a round about 11 in/28 cm in diameter and ⅛ in/3 mm thick. Fit the dough into the pan, pressing it to come 1½ in/4 cm up the sides. (If the dough breaks, just press it together in the pan.) Trim off the excess dough so the dough is flush with the rim of the pan. Spread out the pastry cream in the pan. Drop dollops of the cherry preserves over the pastry cream.

5. Roll out the remaining dough into a round about 9 in/23 cm in diameter and ⅛ in/3 mm thick. Center and fit over the pastry cream. Press the edges of the two dough layers together to enclose the pastry cream and preserves. Using the tines of a fork, score the dough in a crosshatch pattern.

6. Beat the egg yolk and cream together in a small bowl. Brush the dough with the egg mixture.

7. Bake until the dough is golden brown, 40 to 45 minutes. Transfer to a wire cooling rack and let cool completely in the pan.

8. Run a dinner knife around the inside of the pan. If you have a pan with a removable bottom, put the pan on a large can and let the sides fall to the work surface. Otherwise, place a cutting board over the top of the pan. Hold the pan and board together and gently invert to unmold the cake onto the board. Place the serving plate on the bottom of the cake and invert the plate and board together to bring the cake right-side up on the plate. Using a sharp knife, cut into wedges and serve. (The gâteau can be wrapped in plastic wrap and refrigerated for up to 1 day. Let stand at room temperature for 1 hour before serving.)

NOTE: *Almond flour, sometimes called almond meal, comes in two varieties. The less expensive of the two is made from unskinned almonds. The version made from blanched almonds is lighter in color and makes a more delicate-looking crust. The choice is yours, but we use the latter.*

PLUM GALETTE

MAKES 6 TO 8 SERVINGS

Every baker should know how to make a free-form pastry. It is so easy to assemble, doesn't require a pie or tart pan, and can be made with many kinds of fruit. Here is a basic recipe with plums, but try peaches, nectarines, or apricots, too. Stone fruits should be left uncooked, and the dough should be sprinkled with cookie or cake crumbs to soak up the excess juices and keep the delicious crust crisp.

GALETTE DOUGH

2 Tbsp sour cream

2 Tbsp ice-cold water

1 cup/145 g unbleached all-purpose flour, plus more for rolling out the dough

¼ cup/35 g yellow cornmeal

1 tsp sugar

¼ tsp fine sea salt

7 Tbsp/100 g cold unsalted butter, cut into ½-in/12-mm cubes

8 red or Santa Rosa plums, pitted, cut lengthwise into eighths

4 Tbsp/60 g sugar

1 Tbsp cornstarch

1 large egg yolk

1 Tbsp heavy cream or milk

1 Tbsp plus 2 tsp cold unsalted butter, cut into ½-in/12-mm cubes

1. **TO MAKE THE DOUGH:** Mix the sour cream and ice water together in a small bowl. Combine the flour, cornmeal, sugar, and salt in a food processor fitted with the metal blade and pulse a couple of times until combined. Add the butter and pulse about twelve times, until the mixture is crumbly. Turn off the machine, drizzle the sour cream mixture over the flour mixture, and pulse just until the dough comes together. Do not overmix. (Or mix the flour, cornmeal, sugar, and salt in a medium bowl, add the butter, and cut it in with a pastry blender until crumbly. Stir in the sour cream mixture.)

2. Shape the dough into a thick disk and wrap in plastic wrap. Refrigerate until chilled and firm, about 2 hours. The dough is easiest to roll when cold, but not hard. (The dough can be refrigerated for up to 1 day. Let it stand at room temperature for about 15 minutes to soften slightly before rolling.)

3. **TO MAKE THE FILLING:** Position a rack in the center of the oven and preheat to 350°F/180°C/gas 4. Line a rimless baking sheet with parchment paper. (Or turn a large rimmed baking sheet upside down and cover it with parchment paper.)

4. Place the dough on a lightly floured work surface and flour the top of the dough. Roll out the dough into a 13-in/33-cm round about ⅛ in/3 mm thick. Transfer to the lined baking sheet.

5. Toss the plums, 3 Tbsp of the sugar, and the cornstarch in a large bowl. Arrange the plums on the dough in concentric circles, overlapping as needed, leaving a 2-in/5-cm border around the circumference. Fold up the uncovered dough to partially cover the plums, loosely pleating the dough as needed.

6. Beat the egg yolk and cream together in a small bowl.

7. Sprinkle the plums with the remaining 1 Tbsp sugar and the butter. Lightly brush the dough with some of the egg mixture.

CONTINUED

8. Bake until the crust is golden brown, the fruit juices are bubbling, and the bottom is golden brown (lift up with a wide spatula to check), about 35 minutes. Let cool on the baking sheet for 30 minutes. Slide the galette from the baking sheet onto a serving plate. Serve warm or at room temperature.

PEACH OR NECTARINE GALETTE: Replace the plums with 3 ripe peaches or nectarines, peeled, pitted, and sliced ¼ in/6 mm thick. Toss in a bowl with 2 Tbsp sugar and 1 Tbsp cornstarch. Sprinkle 3 Tbsp cake or cookie crumbs (preferably Italian amaretti) in a 9-in/23-cm round in the center of the dough before you add the fruit. Sprinkle the fruit with 1 Tbsp sugar and dot with 1 Tbsp cold butter, cut into small cubes.

CHERRY GALETTE: Replace the plums with 12 oz/340 g Bing cherries, pitted. Toss in a bowl with 2 Tbsp sugar, 1 Tbsp cornstarch, and ⅛ tsp almond extract. Sprinkle 3 Tbsp cake or cookie crumbs (preferably Italian amaretti) in a 9-in/23-cm round in the center of the dough before you add the fruit. Sprinkle the fruit with 1 Tbsp sugar and dot with 1 Tbsp cold butter, cut into small cubes.

PASTRY CREAM

It would be difficult to run a bakery without pastry cream, as it is an important ingredient in many pastries. We use it as a filling for both the Fresh Fruit Tart (page 155) and Gâteau Basque (page 156). Once you learn how to make it, you can whip up a batch in no time.

1½ cups/360 ml whole milk

½ cup/100 g sugar

3 Tbsp cornstarch

5 large egg yolks, at room temperature

2 Tbsp unsalted butter, halved

1 tsp vanilla extract

1. Place a wire sieve over a heat-proof medium bowl and put near the stove. Bring the milk to a simmer in a heavy medium saucepan over medium heat, being careful that the milk doesn't boil over.

2. Meanwhile, whisk the sugar and corn-starch together in a second heat-proof medium bowl. Add the egg yolks and whisk until smooth. Whisk in the hot milk.

3. Return the milk mixture to the sauce-pan. Bring to a full simmer over medium heat, whisking often. Cook for 30 seconds, whisking constantly. (If the pastry cream isn't fully cooked, it could separate when cooled.) Remove from the heat. Add the butter and vanilla and whisk until the but-ter melts. Strain through the sieve. Press a piece of plastic wrap directly on the surface of the pastry cream and pierce a few slits in the plastic with the tip of a sharp knife so the steam can escape. Refrigerate until cooled, about 1 hour. The pastry cream can be stored in the refrigerator for up to 2 days.

WHIPPED CREAM

Many (dare we say all?) desserts are better when topped with a billowy dollop of whipped cream. The cream should be beaten just until it forms soft peaks that barely hold their shape.

1 cup/240 ml heavy cream

2 Tbsp sugar

1 tsp pure vanilla extract

Place a medium bowl in the freezer and freeze until very cold, about 5 minutes. Put the cream, sugar, and vanilla in the bowl. Whip with an electric mixer on high speed until the cream forms soft peaks. Refrigerate until serving. The whipped cream can be prepared up to 8 hours ahead. If it separates, whisk briefly until combined.

LEMON CURD

MAKES ABOUT 1¼ CUPS/340 G

Lemon curd is the star of two of our most popular desserts, Sunny Lemon Cake (page 119), where it is combined with cream, and Lemon Brûlée Tart (page 153). It can also be used on its own as a cake filling or more simply to spread on toast or scones. Practice will teach you how to tell when the curd is done, but an instant-read thermometer will remove the guesswork.

6 large egg yolks

⅓ cup/65 g sugar

⅓ cup/75 ml fresh lemon juice

10 Tbsp/145 g unsalted butter, cut into ½-in/12-mm pieces, at room temperature

1. Place a wire sieve over a heat-proof medium bowl and put near the stove. Whisk the egg yolks, sugar, and lemon juice together in a heavy medium saucepan. Add the butter.

2. Cook, stirring constantly with a heat-proof spatula and scraping down any splashes on the inside of the saucepan, until the butter has melted. Switch to a whisk and whisk constantly until the curd is thick and just short of simmering (an instant-read thermometer inserted in the curd should register 180°F/82°C), about 4 minutes. Do not boil. Immediately strain the curd through the sieve to remove any bits of cooked egg white. Press a piece of plastic wrap directly on the surface of the curd and let cool completely. Transfer to a covered container. Refrigerate until chilled and spreadable, at least 2 hours. The curd can be stored in the refrigerator for up to 5 days.

PIE DOUGH

MAKES ONE 9-IN/23-CM CRUST

Every bakery has a proprietary recipe for pie dough. Our recipe includes butter and vegetable shortening. Since butter tastes so good, why do many recipes use shortening or lard? Unlike butter, these last two fats contain very little water. Since liquid toughens the gluten in flour, the less water in the dough ingredients, the flakier the dough. Ours uses butter and shortening for a light and tender crust, which will improve any pie. For a double-crust pie, just double the recipe.

1½ cups/220 g unbleached all-purpose flour

½ tsp sugar

¼ tsp fine sea salt

5 Tbsp/70 g unsalted butter, cut into ½-in/12-mm cubes, chilled

¼ cup/55 g vegetable shortening, cut into ½-in/12-mm chunks, chilled

¼ cup/60 ml ice-cold water, as needed

1. Whisk the flour, sugar, and salt together in a large bowl. Add the butter and toss to coat with flour. Using a pastry blender, cut the butter into the flour mixture until the pieces are about half their original size. Add the shortening and toss to coat. Continue cutting in the butter and shortening until the mixture looks like coarse bread crumbs with some pea-size pieces of the solids. Do not overmix. While stirring the mixture with a fork, gradually add enough of the water so the dough begins to clump together.

2. Gather up the dough and shape into a thick disk. Wrap in plastic wrap and refrigerate until chilled but not hard, about 1 hour. The dough can be refrigerated for up to 1 day. If the dough is well chilled and hard, let stand at room temperature for about 15 minutes before rolling out.

TART DOUGH

MAKES ONE 9-IN/23-CM CRUST

Pie dough is supposed to be flaky and tender. Tart dough is almost like a cookie and bakes up buttery, crisp, and a bit sweet. Be sure to make it at least an hour before using so the gluten in the flour has time to relax before you roll it out.

½ cup/115 g unsalted butter, at room temperature

⅓ cup/65 g sugar

1 large egg yolk

2 Tbsp whole milk

1¼ cups/165 g cake flour (not self-rising)

¼ tsp fine sea salt

1. Beat the butter in a medium bowl with an electric mixer set on high speed until smooth, about 1 minute. Add the sugar and beat until light in color and texture, about 2 minutes. Beat in the egg yolk, and then dribble in the milk. Reduce the mixer speed to low. Mix the flour and salt together in a small bowl, then gradually add to the butter mixture and mix just until the dough is smooth.

2. Turn out the dough onto a floured work surface. Shape into a thick disk. Wrap in plastic wrap and refrigerate until chilled but not hard, about 1 hour. The dough can be refrigerated for up to 1 day. If the dough is well chilled and hard, let stand at room temperature for about 15 minutes before rolling out.

THE MODEL BAKERY ON PIES AND TARTS

All of the dough ingredients should be cold before mixing. If you are baking in a hot kitchen (as we do 99 percent of the time in St. Helena, where the naturally warm temperature is augmented by the heat of the oven), you can even freeze the dry ingredients and the fats for 30 minutes or so to be sure that everything is chilled. Cold butter and shortening will melt in the hot oven, creating little bursts of steam, which give the dough its flaky texture.

Cornstarch and flour are both reliable thickeners for fruit fillings. If the fruit is naturally acidic, like blueberries, the juices will break down the cornstarch as the pie stands, so flour would be a better choice. Don't be concerned if your pie filling is loose. You just can't tell how much natural pectin the fruit has until after baking. A slightly runny filling is better than one that is too thick and gummy.

Good pies cannot be rushed. The dough must be refrigerated for at least 20 minutes, a rest that relaxes the gluten in the flour and firms the dough so it will be easier to roll out. After the rolled dough is fitted into the pan, it should be frozen for another (shorter) period of relaxing and firming, a step that reduces shrinkage during baking. And finally, most pies need to be completely cooled before serving.

We use aluminum pie pans at the bakery because they are sturdy and hold the oven heat well. At home you may prefer a Pyrex pie plate, which is also an excellent choice because you can see through the pie plate to check how the crust is baking. Metal tart pans with removable bottoms are best for tarts. We also use 5-in/12-cm tartlet pans for individual tarts.

Many fruit-based pie fillings tend to release their juices during baking, and this can make a mess out of your oven floor. Get in the habit of baking pies with the pan on a baking sheet lined with parchment paper or foil. When juices bubble over, the lining can easily be thrown away for a quick cleanup.

There are a couple of ways to ensure a pie or tart crust has a crisp bottom. Prebaking the shell (as we do for the Brandied Pumpkin Pie on page 148) is one method that works well with egg-based pie fillings. Another tip is to bake the pie on a baking sheet, even when you're not expecting the filling to be runny. The hot, flat surface browns the crust more evenly than the wires of an oven rack.

COOKIES

At the Model Bakery, we make sure the entire cookie family is represented every day, so if you visit, you are bound to enjoy a favorite, no matter when you drop in. You'll find bar cookies (our espresso-kissed brownies and gooey carmelitas), drop cookies (like oatmeal-raisin and a couple of different chocolate chip variations), and shaped cookies (Linzer cookies). When a holiday rolls around, the baking team makes rolled sugar cookies cut and decorated into appropriate seasonal shapes: hearts for Valentine's Day, eggs and bunnies for Easter, and everything from stars to trees for Christmas. You'll find recipes for all of them in this chapter. We like to make oversized cookies— if you are only going to have a single cookie, let it be a big one! Feel free to break the cookie into smaller portions as appetites demand.

LEMON SQUARES

MAKES 9 BARS

You may already have a favorite recipe for lemon squares. After all, they are one of America's most beloved cookies, and have been around for years. Our version is not only the best one we know, but the easiest, as it has a simple baked-on topping instead of a separately prepared lemon curd, which many bakers use. You may be surprised at the amount of sugar that is needed to balance the lemon juice. Be forewarned that experiments to reduce the sugar could be disappointing. We've tried!

CRUST

½ cup/115 g unsalted butter, cut into ½-in/12-mm pieces, at room temperature, plus more for the pan

1 cup/145 g unbleached all-purpose flour, plus more for the pan

¼ cup/30 g confectioners' sugar

FILLING

1½ cups/300 g granulated sugar

⅓ cup plus 1 Tbsp/60 g unbleached all-purpose flour

3 large eggs, at room temperature

¼ cup/60 ml fresh lemon juice

Confectioners' sugar for sprinkling

1. **TO MAKE THE CRUST:** Position a rack in the center of the oven and preheat to 350°F/180°C/gas 4. Lightly butter an 8-in/20-cm square baking pan. Dust with flour and tap out the excess.

2. Stir the flour and confectioners' sugar together in a large bowl. Stir in the butter to coat the pieces with the flour mixture. Cut in the butter with a pastry blender (or rub the ingredients together with your fingertips) until the mixture is crumbly. Press the mixture firmly and evenly into the bottom and up the sides of the prepared pan.

3. Bake until the crust is golden brown, 15 to 20 minutes. Remove the pan from the oven. Let stand while making the filling.

4. **TO MAKE THE FILLING:** Whisk the sugar and flour together in a medium bowl. Add the eggs and lemon juice and whisk until smooth. Pour over the hot crust and return to the oven.

5. Bake until the filling is set in the center, about 20 minutes. Let cool completely in the pan on a wire cooling rack. Run a dinner knife around the inside of the pan to loosen the bars. Cut into nine squares. Just before serving, sift confectioners' sugar over the bars. (The cookies can be refrigerated in an airtight container for up to 3 days.)

BROWNIES

MAKES 9 BROWNIES

Many of our customers say that we have the fudgiest, most intensely chocolate brownies in the Valley. Hyperbole aside, they *are* awfully good—thick slabs of dark sweetness enhanced by a bit of espresso. The unusual method of melting the chocolate with a hot butter and sugar mixture is one reason for their irresistibly moist texture.

¾ cup plus 1 Tbsp/185 g unsalted butter, plus more for the pan

Unbleached all-purpose flour for the pan

1 cup/130 g cake flour (not self-rising)

¾ tsp baking powder

¾ tsp fine sea salt

10 oz/280 g semisweet chocolate (no more than 55% cacao), finely chopped

1 cup/200 g sugar

3 Tbsp brewed espresso (or 1½ tsp instant espresso dissolved in 3 Tbsp boiling water)

1 tsp pure vanilla extract

3 large eggs, beaten, at room temperature

1⅓ cups/225 g semisweet chocolate chips

1. Position a rack in the center of the oven and preheat to 350°F/180°C/gas 4. Butter an 8-in/20-cm square baking pan. Line the bottom of the pan with parchment paper. Dust the sides with all-purpose flour and tap out the excess.

2. Sift the cake flour, baking powder, and salt together into a medium bowl. Put the chopped chocolate in a heat-proof medium bowl. Heat the butter, sugar, and espresso together in a medium saucepan over medium heat, stirring often, until the butter is melted. Pour the hot butter mixture over the chocolate and let stand until the chocolate softens, about 1 minute. Add the vanilla and whisk until the chocolate is melted. Gradually beat in the eggs. Add the flour mixture and stir until smooth, making sure to scrape up the chocolate mixture in the bottom of the bowl. Fold in the chocolate chips. Spread out evenly in the prepared pan.

3. Bake until a wooden toothpick inserted in the center comes out clean, about 35 minutes. Let cool completely in the pan on a wire cooling rack. Cut into nine squares. The brownies can be stored in an airtight container at room temperature for up to 5 days.

CARMELITA BARS

MAKES 18 BARS

With a name like carmelita, you can be sure that caramel is going to show up somewhere in this recipe. The original recipe for these gooey, crumb-topped bars was on the back of an oatmeal box and used a jar of caramel sauce. You could do it that way to save time, but the secret of our carmelitas is homemade caramel. Be sure to cook the caramel to the smoking point—any less, and the caramel won't have the bitter note that makes it so delectable.

CARAMEL

2 cups/400 g granulated sugar

½ cup/120 ml water

2 tsp light corn syrup

1 cup/240 ml heavy cream

CRUST

Butter, at room temperature, for the pan

3 cups/255 g old-fashioned (rolled) oats

1⅔ cups/235 g unbleached all-purpose flour, plus more for the pan

¾ cup/150 g packed light brown sugar

½ tsp baking soda

¼ tsp salt

¾ cup/170 unsalted butter, melted

2 Tbsp water

1 cup/170 g semisweet chocolate chips

1 cup/115 g chopped walnuts

1. **TO MAKE THE CARAMEL:** Stir the granulated sugar, water, and corn syrup together in a large heavy saucepan over high heat until the sugar has dissolved. Boil, without stirring, occasionally rotating the pan by the handle to swirl the syrup and washing down any crystals that form on the sides of the pan with a natural-bristle brush dipped in cold water, until the syrup is smoking and the color of old copper, 3 to 5 minutes. Reduce the heat to low.

2. Add the cream (it will bubble up, so be careful) and stir until the caramel is smooth. Remove from the heat and let cool until tepid and thickened, about 1 hour.

3. **TO MAKE THE CRUST:** Position a rack in the center of the oven and preheat to 350°F/180°C/gas 4. Butter and flour a 13-by-9-in/33-by-23-cm baking pan.

4. Whisk the oats, flour, brown sugar, baking soda, and salt together in a large bowl. Stir in the melted butter and water until

the oat mixture is moistened. Transfer about one-fourth of the mixture to a bowl; set aside. Transfer the remainder into the prepared pan and press it firmly and evenly into the bottom of the pan.

5. Bake until the crust is golden brown, 20 to 25 minutes. Remove from the oven. Spread the caramel over the crust. Sprinkle the chocolate chips and walnuts evenly over the caramel. Crumble the reserved oat mixture, as evenly as possible, over the top. Return to the oven and bake until the topping is barely golden brown, about 15 minutes. The chocolate chips should not be completely melted.

6. Let cool completely in the pan on a wire cooling rack. Run a dinner knife around the inside of the pan to loosen the bars. Using a sharp knife, cut into eighteen bars. The cookies can be stored in an airtight container at room temperature for up to 3 days.

CHOCOLATE RADS

MAKES 12 LARGE COOKIES

These radically chocolate cookies are guaranteed to be a hit. When we were putting this book together, many customers made us promise to put this one down on paper. The chocolate is, of course, an important element, but some people are surprised to find espresso in here, as well. We use Guittard's French Vanilla, a not-too-bitter semisweet chocolate with 54 percent cacao content. Some markets in the western United States sell chunks of it in bulk, but any top-quality chocolate with a similar cacao content is fine. Crackly, chewy-soft, and jammed with chocolate, this is one great cookie. You will need a stand mixer to make the sturdy dough.

⅔ cup/95 g unbleached all-purpose flour

2½ tsp baking powder

¼ tsp fine sea salt

1 lb/455 g semisweet chocolate (no more than 55% cacao), finely chopped

4 Tbsp/55 g unsalted butter, at room temperature

1⅔ cups/330 g sugar

4 large eggs, at room temperature

1 Tbsp cold brewed espresso (or 1 tsp instant espresso dissolved in 1 Tbsp boiling water and cooled)

2½ tsp pure vanilla extract

2 cups/340 g semisweet chocolate chips

1 cup/115 g chopped walnuts

1. Sift the flour, baking powder, and salt together into a small bowl and set aside. Put the chopped chocolate in a large heat-proof bowl, preferably stainless steel. Set over a large saucepan of barely simmering water and let stand, stirring occasionally, just until the chocolate is melted and smooth. Remove the bowl from the saucepan and add the butter. Let stand, stirring occasionally, until the butter is melted and incorporated into the chocolate.

2. Beat the sugar and eggs in the bowl of a stand mixer fitted with the whisk attachment on high speed until the mixture is fluffy, thick, and pale yellow, about 5 minutes. (Or whisk the mixture by hand for about 8 minutes.) Beat in the espresso and vanilla.

3. Reduce the mixer speed to low. Add the melted chocolate, being careful not to over-mix. Add the flour mixture, stopping to scrape the sides and bottom of the bowl to ensure that the batter is completely mixed. Stir in the chocolate chips and walnuts. The dough will be soft, so let it stand until firm enough to shape, 20 to 30 minutes.

4. Place an 18-by-13-in/46-by-33-cm sheet of parchment paper on the work surface. Drop large spoonfuls of the dough across the width of the paper. Using wet hands, pat and shape the dough into a 12-by-3-in/30.5-by-7.5-cm log. Wrap the dough in the parchment paper, smoothing the dough into an even log. Twist the ends of the paper closed. Place the log on a baking sheet and refrigerate until firm enough to slice, at least 2 hours or up to 1 day.

CONTINUED

COOKIES

5. Position racks in the top third and center of the oven and preheat to 350°F/180°C/gas 4. Line two half-sheet pans with parchment paper.

6. Since the log will be flat where it sat on the baking sheet, roll the wrapped dough on the work surface to smooth it so that the slices will be nice and round. Unwrap the dough. Using a thin, sharp knife dipped in water, cut the dough into twelve 1-in-/2.5-cm-thick rounds. Arrange the rounds about 3 in/7.5 cm apart on the lined pans, allowing four cookies per pan. Refrigerate the remaining rounds.

7. Bake, switching the position of the pans from top to bottom and front to back halfway through baking, until the tops of the cookies are cracked and the edges are beginning to crisp, about 20 minutes. Let cool on the pans for 5 minutes. Transfer to wire cooling racks and let cool completely. Repeat with the remaining dough rounds on a cooled pan. The cookies can be stored in an airtight container at room temperature for up to 3 days.

ALMOND MACAROONS

MAKES 12 LARGE COOKIES

Our friend Molly Chappellet, a cookbook writer as well as the female head of one of the Valley's pioneering wine families, absolutely loves these chewy almond cookies. The Chappellet family is one of the few nonrestaurant accounts we maintain at the bakery, and we can't begin to count the dozens of cookies they have purchased over the decades. Our recipe uses 1 lb/455 g of almond paste, and it will be much less pricey to make if you buy the paste in bulk instead of in cans at the supermarket. A couple of important tips: Make sure the cookie dough stands for at least 30 minutes before scooping, and let the cookies cool completely on the pans before you remove them, or they will stick to it.

---

1 lb/455 g almond paste, broken into walnut-size chunks

1½ cups/300 g granulated sugar

4 large egg whites, at room temperature

⅔ cup/80 g confectioners' sugar, sifted

¼ cup/35 g unbleached all-purpose flour

1. Process the almond paste and granulated sugar in a food processor fitted with the metal blade to make fine crumbs. Add the egg whites, confectioners' sugar, and flour and process until the dough comes together. Scrape out of the food processor into a medium bowl. Cover with plastic wrap and refrigerate for at least 30 minutes or up to 4 hours before baking.

2. Position racks in the top third and center of the oven and preheat to 350°F/180°C/gas 4. Line two half-sheet pans with parchment paper.

3. Using a number-16 food-portion scoop with about a ¼-cup/60-ml capacity for each cookie, drop scoops of the dough onto the lined pans, placing them about 2 in/5 cm apart. You should be able to fit six cookies on each pan.

4. Bake, switching the positions of the pans from top to bottom and front to back halfway through baking, until the cookies are golden brown and fully risen in the center, about 25 minutes. Let cool completely on the pans. Carefully remove the cookies from the pan. The cookies can be stored in an airtight container at room temperature for up to 5 days.

OATMEAL-RAISIN COOKIES

MAKES 18 LARGE COOKIES

When Alex places a personal bakery order with his nana, Karen, he usually asks her to bring home "the raisin ones." You will understand why they are one of his favorites. These are the ultimate cookie jar filler—just the thing to whip together in a few minutes with ingredients that you are likely to have on hand, and guaranteed to please everyone who eats them.

2 cups/290 g unbleached all-purpose flour

1 tsp baking soda

1 tsp ground cinnamon

¾ tsp fine sea salt

⅛ tsp freshly grated nutmeg

1 cup/225 g unsalted butter, at room temperature

2 cups/400 g packed light brown sugar

2 large eggs, at room temperature

1 tsp pure vanilla extract

2 cups/190 g old-fashioned (rolled) oats

1 cup/170 g dark raisins

1. Position racks in the top third and center of the oven and preheat to 350°F/180°C/gas 4. Line two half-sheet pans with parchment paper.

2. Sift the flour, baking soda, cinnamon, salt, and nutmeg together into a medium bowl. Beat the butter and brown sugar together in a large bowl with an electric mixer set on medium speed, occasionally scraping down the sides of the bowl, until light in color, about 3 minutes. (Or cream the butter and sugar together in a large bowl with a wooden spoon until light in color, about 5 minutes.) Beat in the eggs, one at a time, and then the vanilla. Reduce the mixer speed to low. Add the flour mixture in thirds, mixing just until combined. Stir in the oats and raisins.

3. Using a number-16 food-portion scoop with about a ¼-cup/60-ml capacity, drop scoops of dough onto the lined pans, spacing them about 2 in/5 cm apart. You will only be able to fit six cookies on each pan.

4. Bake, switching the pans from top to bottom and front to back halfway through baking, until the cookies are lightly golden and set around the edges, about 15 minutes. Let the cookies cool on the pans for 5 minutes, then transfer to wire cooling racks and let cool completely. Repeat with the remaining dough on cooled pans. The cookies can be stored in an airtight container at room temperature for up to 5 days.

PEANUT BUTTER COOKIES

MAKES ABOUT 18 COOKIES

The perfect peanut butter cookie—crumbly around the edges, but chewy in the middle—came to us via the late Marion Cunningham, who most people learned to love through her thorough retooling of *The Fannie Farmer Cookbook*. Marion was born and bred in California, and for many years she spearheaded "the Baker's Dozen," a group of passionate cooks that included Karen. Thanks, Marion, for sharing your cookie with us and with the hundreds of Model Bakery customers who enjoy it every week.

---

3 cups/435 g all-purpose flour

2 tsp baking soda

¼ tsp salt

1 cup/225 g unsalted butter, at room temperature

1 cup/200 g packed light brown sugar

1 cup/200 g granulated sugar

2 large eggs, at room temperature

1 cup/255 g chunky peanut butter

1. Position racks in the top third and center of the oven and preheat to 350°F/180°C/gas 4. Line two half-sheet pans with parchment paper.

2. Sift the flour, baking soda, and salt together into a medium bowl. Beat the butter, brown sugar, and granulated sugar together in a large bowl with an electric mixer set on high speed just until smooth and beginning to turn pale, about 1½ minutes. (Or cream the butter and sugars together in a large bowl with a wooden spoon until beginning to turn pale, about 3 minutes.) Beat in the eggs, one at a time. Beat in the peanut butter. Reduce the mixer speed to low. Gradually add the flour mixture, mixing just until combined.

3. Using a number-16 food-portion scoop with about a ¼-cup/60-ml capacity, drop scoops of the dough onto the lined pans, spacing them about 2 in/5 cm apart. You should be able to fit about six cookies on each pan.

4. Bake, switching the pans from top to bottom and front to back halfway through baking, until the cookies are very lightly browned around the edges, 15 to 18 minutes. Let the cookies cool on the pans for 5 minutes, then transfer to wire cooling racks and let cool completely. Repeat with the remaining dough on cooled pans. The cookies can be stored in an airtight container at room temperature for up to 5 days.

THE ULTIMATE CHOCOLATE CHIP COOKIES

MAKES 16 LARGE COOKIES

These are the chocolate chip cookies of your dreams—that is, if you like them big, chewy, and filled with chips and nuts. Most traditional recipes for this cookie use granulated sugar in addition to the brown sugar, but it's the brown sugar that supplies the moisture. With all due respect, fans of thin, crisp chocolate chip cookies should look elsewhere.

---

2 cups/290 g unbleached all-purpose flour

¾ tsp baking soda

½ tsp fine sea salt

¾ cup plus 1 Tbsp/185 g unsalted butter, at room temperature

1⅓ cups/275 g packed light brown sugar

2 large eggs, at room temperature

1 tsp pure vanilla extract

2⅔ cups/450 g chocolate chips

1 cup/115 g chopped walnuts

1. Position racks in the top third and center of the oven and preheat to 375°F/190°C/gas 5. Line two half-sheet pans with parchment paper.

2. Sift the flour, baking soda, and salt together into a medium bowl. Beat the butter and brown sugar together in a large bowl with an electric mixer set on medium speed, occasionally scraping down the sides of the bowl, until light in color, about 1½ minutes. (Or cream the butter and sugar together in a large bowl with a wooden spoon until light in color, about 5 minutes.) Beat in the eggs, one at a time, and then the vanilla. Reduce the mixer speed to low. Add the flour mixture in thirds, mixing just until combined. Stir in the chocolate chips and walnuts.

3. Using a number-16 food-portion scoop with about a ¼-cup/60-ml capacity, drop scoops of dough onto the lined pans, spacing them about 3 in/7.5 cm apart. You will only be able to fit three or four cookies on each pan.

4. Bake, switching the pans from top to bottom and front to back halfway through baking, until the cookies are lightly golden and set around the edges, 14 to 17 minutes. Let the cookies cool on the pans for 5 minutes, then transfer to wire cooling racks and let cool completely. Repeat with the remaining dough on cooled pans. The cookies can be stored in an airtight container at room temperature for up to 5 days.

WHITE CHOCOLATE CHIP AND HAZELNUT COOKIES

MAKES 15 LARGE COOKIES

Here is a variation on the chocolate chip theme that vanilla lovers (you know who you are) will appreciate. Whenever you shop for white chocolate, look carefully at the label and make sure it lists cocoa butter. If palm oil or other tropical fats have been used, skip it.

2⅓ cups/340 g unbleached all-purpose flour

1 tsp baking soda

½ tsp fine sea salt

11 Tbsp/160 g unsalted butter, at room temperature

¾ cup/150 g packed light brown sugar

¾ cup/150 g granulated sugar

2 large eggs, at room temperature

2 Tbsp water

2 tsp pure vanilla extract

2 cups/340 g white chocolate chips

⅔ cup/90 g toasted, skinned, and chopped hazelnuts (see page 30)

1. Position racks in the top third and center of the oven and preheat to 350°F/180°C/gas 4. Line two half-sheet pans with parchment paper.

2. Sift the flour, baking soda, and salt together into a medium bowl. Beat the butter, brown sugar, and granulated sugar together in a large bowl with an electric mixer set on medium speed, occasionally scraping down the sides of the bowl, until light in color, about 3 minutes. (Or cream the butter and sugars together in a large bowl with a wooden spoon until light in color, about 5 minutes.) Beat in the eggs, one at a time, and then the water and vanilla. Reduce the mixer speed to low. Add the flour mixture in thirds, mixing just until combined. Stir in the white chocolate chips and hazelnuts.

3. Using a number-16 food-portion scoop with about a ¼-cup/60-ml capacity, drop scoops of the dough onto the lined pans, spacing them about 3 in/7.5 cm apart. You will only be able to fit three or four cookies on each pan.

4. Bake, switching the pans from top to bottom and front to back halfway through baking, until the cookies are lightly golden and set around the edges, about 17 minutes. Let the cookies cool on the pans for 5 minutes, then transfer to wire cooling racks and let cool completely. Repeat with the remaining dough on cooled pans. The cookies can be stored in an airtight container at room temperature for up to 5 days.

TENDER SUGAR COOKIES

MAKES ABOUT 48 COOKIES

Here is a simple but delicious sugar cookie with a melt-in-your-mouth texture that is perfect with a cup of afternoon tea. For Christmas cookies, roll them in cinnamon-sugar or colored sugar. Because it is so popular with the younger set, we call this "the kid's cookie."

4⅔ cups/610 g cake flour (not self-rising)

1½ tsp baking soda

1½ tsp cream of tartar

1 cup/225 g unsalted butter, at room temperature

1½ cups/300 g granulated sugar

1¼ cups/145 g confectioners' sugar, sifted

1 cup/240 ml vegetable oil

2 large eggs, at room temperature

½ tsp pure vanilla extract

1. Sift the flour, baking soda, and cream of tartar together into a large bowl. Mix the butter, 1 cup/200 g of the granulated sugar, and the confectioners' sugar together in the bowl of a stand mixer on low speed, just until combined. Increase the speed to high and beat, occasionally scraping down the sides of the bowl, until light in color, about 2 minutes. Gradually beat in the vegetable oil. (Or cream the butter and sugars together in a large bowl with a wooden spoon until beginning to turn pale, about 3 minutes. Gradually whisk in the oil.) Beat in the eggs, one at a time, mixing well after each addition and scraping down the sides of the bowl as needed. Mix in the vanilla. Reduce the mixer speed to low. Add the flour mixture in thirds and mix to make a soft dough. Cover the bowl with plastic wrap and refrigerate until the dough is firm enough to scoop, at least 2 hours or up to 1 day.

2. Position racks in the top third and center of the oven and preheat to 350°F/180°C/gas 4. Line two half-sheet pans with parchment paper.

3. Using about 1 Tbsp for each cookie, roll the dough into about forty-eight balls. Put the remaining ½ cup/100 g granulated sugar in a bowl. Dip just one side of each ball in the sugar. Arrange the balls, sugar-side up, about 1 in/2.5 cm apart (the cookies don't spread much) on the lined pans.

4. Bake, switching the pans from top to bottom and front to back halfway through baking, until the cookies are barely golden and set around the edges, 12 to 15 minutes. Do not overbake. Let the cookies cool on the pans for 5 minutes, then transfer to wire cooling racks and let cool completely. The cookies can be stored in an airtight container at room temperature for up to 5 days.

FESTIVE SUGAR COOKIES

MAKES ABOUT 36 COOKIES

At every major holiday (and even some not so major, like Bastille Day) we roll, cut, and decorate thousands of gorgeous sugar cookies, which taste as good as they look. (We do not exaggerate—we sold more than ten thousand cookies last December.) Our dough is easy to handle, crisp yet tender, and, of course, tasty. The cookies are dipped in our signature shiny icing to give them a smooth surface, which can be left plain or be further embellished with royal icing or other frosting. A disposable plastic pastry bag, with the tip snipped off, makes the perfect tool for piping. For the simplest decorations, apply holiday candies, colored sugars, or sprinkles to iced cookies. Let your imagination go.

---

5 cups/725 g unbleached all-purpose flour, plus more for rolling out the dough

1 tsp fine sea salt

1 lb/455 g unsalted butter, at room temperature

1½ cups/300 g sugar

2 large eggs, beaten, at room temperature

1 tsp pure vanilla extract

1 recipe Shiny Cookie Icing (page 187)

1 recipe Royal Icing (page 187)

1. Sift the flour and salt together into a medium bowl. Beat the butter in a large bowl with an electric mixer set on high speed until the butter is smooth, about 1 minute. Gradually beat in the sugar and continue beating until light in color and texture, occasionally scraping down the sides of the bowl with a rubber spatula, about 2 minutes. (Or cream the butter and sugar together in a large bowl with a wooden spoon until light in color, about 8 minutes.) Beat in the eggs, one at a time, beating well after each addition to be sure they are thoroughly absorbed into the butter mixture. Beat in the vanilla. Reduce the mixer speed to low. Gradually mix in the flour mixture, scraping down the sides of the bowl as needed, until the dough comes together.

2. Gather up the dough and divide it into thirds. Wrap each portion in parchment paper or plastic wrap. Refrigerate until

chilled and firm, at least 2 hours or up to 2 days. (The dough can be frozen, wrapped in plastic wrap and an overwrap of aluminum foil, for up to 1 month. Defrost in the refrigerator overnight.)

3. Position racks in the top third and center of the oven and preheat to 350°F/180°C/gas 4. Line two half-sheet pans with parchment paper.

4. Let the dough stand at room temperature for about 15 minutes to soften slightly without losing its chill. Working with one portion of dough at a time, place the unwrapped dough on a lightly floured work surface and dust the top of the dough with flour. Roll out the dough until ¼ in/6 mm thick. (If the dough is thinner than this, it tends to leave crumbs in the icing during glazing.) Using cookie cutters, cut out the shapes of your choice. Arrange the cookies 1 in/2.5 cm apart on the lined pans. The

CONTINUED

scraps can be gathered up and gently kneaded together, and then rolled and cut out until the dough is used up.

5. Bake, switching the pans from top to bottom and front to back halfway through baking, until the edges of the cookies are lightly browned, 12 to 15 minutes. Let the cookies cool on the pans for 5 minutes, then transfer to wire cooling racks and let cool completely. (The undecorated cookies can be stored in airtight containers at room temperature for up to 2 days.)

6. Line at least one half-sheet pan with parchment or waxed paper. Set a large wire cooling rack in the pan.

7. Pour the shiny cookie icing into a small, deep heat-proof (stainless-steel or Pyrex) bowl. Holding a cookie smooth-side down (that is, with the side that touched the baking sheet facing up), dip just the cookie's "face" onto the surface of the icing to coat it. Let the excess icing drip back into the bowl and clean the sides of the cookie

with your forefinger. Place on the cooling rack. Repeat with the remaining cookies and icing. (If the icing firms up or forms a crust, place the bowl in a skillet of gently simmering water and stir the icing until it is fluid again, taking care not to splash water into the icing.) Let the cookies stand until the icing is completely set.

8. Put the royal icing in a small disposable plastic pastry bag, squeezing the icing into the tip of the bag. Using scissors, snip off the tip to make a $\frac{1}{16}$-in/2-mm opening in the tip of the bag. Pipe line decorations as desired onto the glazed cookies. Let stand until the decorations are firm. The cookies can be stored, stacked and separated with parchment or wax paper, in airtight containers at room temperature for up to 5 days.

SHINY COOKIE ICING

MAKES ABOUT 2¼ CUPS/103 KG,
ENOUGH FOR ABOUT 72 COOKIES

Many bakeries rely on egg white–based royal icing for giving cookies a glossy glaze. We have developed an egg-free alternative, which we affectionately nicknamed "goop," because that's what it is! It can be made ahead and refrigerated, to use as needed—a boon during the busy holiday cookie seasons, when we have buckets of goop in the walk-in refrigerator, marked by color.

8 cups/920 g confectioners' sugar (no need to sift)

½ cup/115 g unsalted butter

½ cup/120 ml whole milk, plus more as needed

2 Tbsp light corn syrup

Put the confectioners' sugar in a large bowl. Heat the butter and milk together in a medium saucepan over medium heat, stirring until the milk is hot and steaming (the butter does not have to be completely melted). Using an electric mixer set on low speed, gradually beat the hot milk mixture into the confectioners' sugar, scraping down the sides of the bowl often. Continue mixing until smooth. Add the corn syrup and beat until smooth and shiny. If necessary, add more milk, 1 tsp at a time, until the icing has the consistency of housepaint. Cover the bowl with plastic wrap until ready to use. The icing can be made up to 5 days ahead. Store, covered, in the refrigerator. To use, transfer the icing to a heat-proof bowl, preferably stainless steel. Place the bowl in a skillet of gently simmering water, stirring the icing occasionally and taking care not to splash water into the icing, just until warmed and fluid enough for dipping.

ROYAL ICING

MAKES ABOUT 2 CUPS/500 G,
ENOUGH FOR ABOUT 72 COOKIES

Royal icing is used to pipe line decorations onto glazed cookies. The traditional icing uses raw egg whites, but the dried egg white powder in this recipe is a salmonella-safe option and is available at many supermarkets and online. If you wish, substitute 3 egg whites, or the equivalent in pasteurized egg whites, which are available in the refrigerated section of the supermarket, for the dried egg white powder and water.

4 cups/455 g confectioners' sugar, sifted

¼ cup plus 2 Tbsp/90 ml water

2 Tbsp dried egg white powder

1 tsp fresh lemon juice

In a medium bowl, using an electric mixer at low speed, mix the confectioners' sugar, water, egg white powder, and lemon juice until combined. Increase the speed to high and beat, scraping down the sides of the bowl often, until very stiff, shiny, and thick enough to pipe, 3 to 5 minutes. Cover with a wet paper towel pressed directly onto the surface of the icing until ready to use to avoid crusting. The icing can be stored in an airtight container in the refrigerator, with a moist paper towel on the surface, for up to 2 days.

RASPBERRY LINZER COOKIES

MAKES ABOUT 28 SANDWICH COOKIES

The Austrian city of Linz is famous for Linzer torte, a tartlike pastry with a nut–based dough and a filling of fruit preserves—a flavor combination that is wonderful in sandwich cookies, too. We cut the dough into hearts for Valentine's Day, and for Christmas, our wreath–shaped Linzer cookies are a charming addition to a cookie tray.

2 cups/230 g sliced natural almonds

2¼ cups/325 g unbleached all-purpose flour, plus more for rolling out the dough

1¼ cups/280 g unsalted butter, at room temperature

⅔ cup/130 g granulated sugar

2 tsp pure vanilla extract

Grated zest of 1 lemon

1 cup/300 g raspberry preserves

Confectioners' sugar for sprinkling

1. Process the almonds and ½ cup/75 g of the flour in a food processor fitted with the metal blade until the nuts are very finely ground. Transfer to a medium bowl and add the remaining 1¾ cups/250 g flour.

2. Beat the butter in a large bowl with an electric mixer set on medium speed until smooth, about 1 minute. Gradually beat in the granulated sugar and continue beating until light in color and texture, about 1 minute. (Or cream the butter and granulated sugar together in a large bowl with a wooden spoon until beginning to turn pale, about 3 minutes.) Beat in the vanilla and lemon zest. Reduce the mixer speed to low. Add the flour mixture in thirds and mix just until smooth.

3. Shape the dough into two thick disks. Wrap each portion in plastic wrap. Refrigerate until chilled and firm, at least 2 hours or up to 2 days. (If the dough is very hard, let stand for about 15 minutes to soften slightly before rolling.)

4. Position racks in the top third and center of the oven and preheat to 350°F/180°C/gas 4. Line two half–sheet pans with parchment paper.

5. Working with one disk of dough at a time, roll out the dough on a lightly floured work surface until ⅛ in/3 mm thick. Using a 2½-in/6-cm fluted cookie cutter, cut out rounds of dough. Arrange the cookies about 1 in/2.5 apart on the lined pans. Reroll the scraps until all of the dough has been used, refrigerating the dough as needed. You should have about sixty rounds.

6. Using a 1–in/2.5–cm fluted cookie cutter, cut the centers from half of the cookies to make the cookie tops. The whole cookies will be the bottoms. Bake, switching the pans from top to bottom and front to back halfway through baking, until the edges of the cookies are very lightly browned, about 15 minutes. Let the cookies cool on the pans for 5 minutes, then transfer to wire cooling racks and let cool completely.

7. Spread about 1 tsp of the preserves on each whole cookie. Sift confectioners' sugar over the cookie tops. Sandwich on the bottoms and press gently to adhere. The cookies can be stored in an airtight container at room temperature, with the layers separated by wax or parchment paper, for up to 5 days.

GINGER MOLASSES COOKIES

MAKES ABOUT 18 LARGE COOKIES

These big, soft, old-fashioned treats have a reputation for being the best ginger cookies in California. Even the *Los Angeles Times*, not a local paper by any means, has asked for our recipe. Many ginger cookie recipes call for melted butter, and we used to make them that way. But they were too delicate, and when we changed to creamed butter, chewy perfection was ours. You will only be able to fit three or four cookies on a half-sheet pan, so plan accordingly.

4 cups/580 g unbleached all-purpose flour

2 tsp ground cinnamon

1 tsp ground cloves

1 tsp ground ginger

1 tsp baking soda

1 tsp fine sea salt

1½ cups/300 g granulated sugar

1⅓ cups/300 g unsalted butter

½ cup/120 ml unsulfured molasses (not blackstrap)

2 large eggs at room temperature

1 tsp pure vanilla extract

½ cup/100 g demerara or raw sugar

1. Sift the flour, cinnamon, cloves, ginger, baking soda, and salt together into a large bowl. Beat the granulated sugar and butter together in a large bowl with an electric mixer set on medium speed, occasionally scraping down the sides of the bowl, until light in color, about 2 minutes. (Or cream the sugar and butter together in a large bowl with a wooden spoon until light in color, about 5 minutes.) Gradually beat in the molasses. Beat in the eggs, one at a time, and then the vanilla. Reduce the mixer speed to low. Add the flour mixture in thirds and mix to make a soft dough. Cover the bowl with plastic wrap and refrigerate until the dough is firm enough to scoop, at least 2 hours or up to 1 day.

2. Position racks in the top third and center of the oven and preheat to 350°F/180°C/gas 4. Line two half-sheet pans with parchment paper.

3. Using a number-16 food-portion scoop with about a ¼-cup/60-ml capacity, scoop out the dough, dividing it into 16 portions. Roll each into a ball. Put the demerara sugar in a shallow bowl and dip just one side of each ball in the sugar. Arrange the balls, sugar-side up, about 3 in/7.5 cm apart on the lined pans. You will only be able to fit three or four cookies on each pan.

4. Bake, switching the pans from top to bottom and front to back halfway through baking, until the cookies have cracked tops and are set around the edges, 15 to 18 minutes. Let the cookies cool on the pans for 5 minutes, transfer to wire cooling racks and then cool completely. The cookies can be stored in an airtight container at room temperature for up to 5 days.

GINGERBREAD COOKIES

MAKES ABOUT 66 COOKIES

What is Christmas without gingerbread cookies? Our recipe is good and spicy. Your cookie is a blank canvas for you to express your creativity, so have fun when you decorate them, as we do at the bakery with Royal Icing (page 187) and bits of candy for buttons. The exact number of cookies depends, of course, on the size of your cutter. Ours average 3½ in/9 cm across.

5 cups/725 g unbleached all-purpose flour, plus more for rolling out the dough

2 Tbsp ground ginger

2 tsp baking soda

2 tsp ground cinnamon

2 tsp freshly grated nutmeg

1 tsp ground allspice

1 tsp fine sea salt

1 cup/225 g unsalted butter, at room temperature

1 cup/200 g packed light brown sugar

1 cup/240 ml unsulfured molasses (not blackstrap)

2 large eggs, at room temperature

1. Sift the flour, ginger, baking soda, cinnamon, nutmeg, allspice, and salt together into a large bowl. Beat the butter and brown sugar together in a large bowl with an electric mixer set on medium speed just until combined, about 1 minute. (Or cream the butter and sugar together in a large bowl with a wooden spoon until light in color, about 3 minutes.) Gradually beat in the molasses. Beat in the eggs, one at a time. Reduce the mixer speed to low. Gradually add the flour mixture, scraping down the sides of the bowl occasionally, mixing just until combined.

2. Divide the dough in half. Wrap each portion in plastic wrap or aluminum foil. Refrigerate until chilled and firm, at least 4 hours or up to 3 days.)

3. Position racks in the top third and center of the oven and preheat to 350°F/180°C/gas 4. Line two half-sheet pans with parchment paper.

4. Let the dough stand at room temperature for 15 minutes to soften slightly without losing its chill. Working with one portion of dough at a time, place the unwrapped dough on a lightly floured work surface. Roll out the dough until ¼ in/6 mm thick. Using a cookie cutter, cut out cookies and arrange them 1 in/2.5 cm apart on the lined pans.

5. Bake, switching the pans from top to bottom and front to back halfway through baking, until the cookies are just beginning to brown around the edges, about 12 minutes, depending on the size of the cookies. For crisp cookies, bake a few minutes longer. Let the cookies cool on the pans for 3 minutes, then transfer to wire cooling racks and let cool completely.

OUR GINGERBREAD HOUSE

MAKES 1 GINGERBREAD HOUSE

Every December, young and old alike await the arrival of a lovingly handmade gingerbread house in the front window of our St. Helena store. We take over a week to make and decorate it, and use bags of brightly colored candies. No doubt about it, it is a labor of love! Alex, Sarah's son, helps too, as he meticulously applies shredded wheat cereal to the roof (and sneaks a few bites of the candy). Here we provide the pattern for a modestly sized gingerbread house for a fun weekend project. The complexity of your house will be limited only by your imagination and patience.

---

2 recipes Gingerbread Cookie dough (see page 191)

Unbleached all-purpose flour for rolling out the dough

2 recipes Royal Icing (page 187)

Assorted candies for decorating (see page 195)

SPECIAL EQUIPMENT

Boxes, such as cereal or facial tissue boxes, for propping up the walls of the house

2 heavy-duty white cake cardboards or 1 composite cake board, measuring 19 by 13 in/48 by 33 cm (see page 195)

1. Use the illustrated measurements on page 198 to create templates on cardboard or manila paper, and cut them out.

2. At least 2 days before decorating the gingerbread house, bake the gingerbread pieces. Preheat the oven to 350°F/180°C/gas 4. Line two perfectly flat (not warped) half-sheet pans with parchment paper.

3. Divide the gingerbread dough into four equal portions. Working with one portion at a time, let the dough stand at room temperature for about 10 minutes before rolling it out (keep the remaining dough refrigerated). Place the dough on a lightly floured work surface and dust the top with flour. Using a long, heavy rolling pin, roll out the dough until ¼ in/6 mm thick. Using the templates, cut out as many pieces of the house as will fit on the two pans. (Or roll and cut all of the gingerbread dough at once, refrigerating the cut gingerbread pieces on half-sheet pans until ready to bake.) Cut out the door and windows, if desired. Cut

the window pieces in half to use as shutters, setting them aside with the door piece. If you wish, reroll the scraps and cut out gingerbread people to populate your house and yard. Using a wide metal spatula, transfer the cut cookie pieces, including the door and window cutouts, to the lined pans.

4. Bake, switching the pans from top to bottom and front to back halfway through baking, until the dough is crisp and firm (not soft), about 15 minutes for the smaller pieces and about 20 minutes for the larger ones. While the pieces are still warm, cover with their corresponding templates. Use a serrated knife to carefully trim any parts of the cookie that have expanded beyond the template. The pieces should have straight sides so they will fit together well. Let the cookies cool completely on the pans before removing. Continue baking the remaining dough on cool pans and trimming the pieces. Let the cookies stand, uncovered, at room temperature for at least 12 hours before proceeding.

CONTINUED

5. Transfer about one-third of the icing to a pastry bag fitted with a ⅛-in/3-mm plain tip. Decorate the shutters with candy, attaching it with the icing, and let dry. Attach the shutters to the walls with icing and let dry.

6. Pipe icing along the sides of the front wall. Attach the side walls and prop them up with small boxes. Let stand until the icing sets. Apply more icing on the insides of the joints for added strength. Let stand until the icing is fully set, at least 1 hour.

7. Using the icing, attach the back wall to the side walls, piping additional icing on the insides of the joints. Prop in place with small boxes and let stand until the icing is completely set, at least 2 hours or preferably overnight.

8. Transfer more icing to the pastry bag fitted with the same tip. Be sure the half-built house is very solid, and add more icing at the joints, if needed. Pipe a generous line of icing on the cardboard to match the footprint of the house. Place the house on the icing to secure it to the board. Attach the door to the doorway with more icing.

9. Pipe icing along the top edges of the walls on one side of the house. Position one roof piece in place on top of the house, supporting it with a tall box. Let stand until the icing is set, at least 1 hour. Repeat with the remaining roof piece, piping icing where the two pieces meet at the crest of the house. Let the house stand overnight until completely dry.

10. Using the icing, attach the candies to the house, decorating it in a whimsical and colorful manner. Have fun, take your time, and don't eat too many candies!

GINGERBREAD HOUSES

Rome wasn't built in a day. Gingerbread houses are certainly not built in a day either. The best way to make a gingerbread house is to take a very leisurely pace. Make the dough a couple of days ahead (or better yet, make it a week ahead and freeze it). Take your time choosing the candies and other goodies for decorating. Roll out the dough and bake the pieces, and set them aside for another day or so. Once the walls are assembled, they must be allowed to dry completely (overnight) before attaching the roof.

Be sure your baking sheets are flat and not warped—curved pans will make curved cookies, which are difficult to cement together. If you have room in your refrigerator, chill the cookie cutouts before baking to reduce spreading during baking. Or, if the weather is cold, put the pans on a porch to chill.

When it comes to making gingerbread houses, the more half-sheet pans, the better. That way you won't have to wait until the cookies cool on the pans to remove them, and then wait until the pans are cool to position the next batch of dough. A minimum of four half-sheet pans is ideal.

You'll need a solid base for holding the gingerbread house. Rectangular cake boards, measuring 19 by 13 in/48 by 33 cm, made from sturdy cardboard or composite material, are perfect. (You may want to glue two cardboard boards together for a heavier double-thick base.) Cover the board with cake decorators' aluminum foil or colored Christmas paper, if you wish.

Royal icing has a tendency to take a long time to dry when you are in a hurry (and to harden and plug up the pastry tip when you want the icing to flow). You can speed up drying with a handheld electric hair dryer, but nothing beats time. We have cheated and used a glue gun and glue sticks to attach heavier pieces of gingerbread. If you go that route, you can cover the glue seams with royal icing when you attach the candies. Remember, no one eats a gingerbread house—except in fairy tales. When not using the icing in the bag, cover the tip with a wet paper towel to keep the tip opening moist and prevent the icing from drying. If you are not using the icing for long periods of time, transfer it from the pastry bag to a covered container and refrigerate it.

Start your search for interesting, colorful candies to decorate the house early in the season. The best place to look is at a store that sells old-fashioned candies, or search online (see Resources, page 199). If necessary, cut the candies in half horizontally so they fit flat against the walls. Our favorite decorating candies include peppermint (sticks and rounds), M&M's, lemon drops, Life Savers, gum drops, Hershey's Kisses, and hot cinnamon candies. You may also want miniature marshmallows, silver dragées, miniature pretzels, and red or black licorice sticks, whips, and rounds.

Here are some more ideas: For roof shingles, use sugared mini–shredded wheat cereal, white or chocolate candy coating wafers, whole coffee beans (plain or chocolate-covered), or wafer candies, such as Necco's. Use small Tootsie Rolls to make a stack of logs along a wall. Candy rocks can be used to build a stone fence around the house or outline a path to the door. A snow person, with hat and all, can be created out of balls of marzipan or rolled fondant. Make trees by turning pointed ice cream cones upside down and covering them with lines of green royal icing to resemble branches, or use a small leaf tip for a similar effect. Sprinkle the trees with colored nonpareils to simulate colored holiday lights. Spread a thin layer of royal icing on the board and sprinkle with clear sanding sugar to resemble snow.

MERINGUE MUSHROOMS

MAKES ABOUT 48 MERINGUES

We usually make these faux fungi as decorations for the Bûche de Noël (page 125), but they are just as intriguing as cookies on a holiday platter. For the crispiest mushrooms, let the meringues cool and dry overnight in the turned-off oven. If you're making a bûche, be sure to save some ganache to glue the caps and stems together.

1⅓ cups/265 g sugar

½ cup/120 ml water

3 large egg whites, at room temperature

¼ teaspoon cream of tartar

Pinch of fine sea salt

½ cup/120 ml ganache (see page 125) or melted chocolate

Cocoa powder for dusting

1. Position racks in the top third and center of the oven and preheat to 200°F/95°C. Line two half-sheet pans with parchment paper.

2. Bring the sugar and water to a boil in a heavy medium saucepan over high heat, stirring until the sugar dissolves. Attach a candy thermometer to the saucepan. Boil, without stirring, until the syrup reaches 240°F/115°C (soft-ball stage) on the thermometer.

3. Toward the end of the boiling period, whip the egg whites, cream of tartar, and salt in the bowl of a stand mixer fitted with the whisk attachment on high speed just until soft peaks form. When the syrup is ready, with the mixer on high speed, gradually pour the hot syrup into the whipped egg whites in a steady stream, being careful not to pour the syrup directly into the whisk wires or down the sides of the bowl. Beat until the meringue forms stiff, shiny peaks.

4. Transfer the meringue to a pastry bag fitted with a ⅜-in/1-cm plain round tip. On one lined pan, using about two-thirds of the meringue, pipe out about four dozen "mushroom caps," about 2 in/5 cm in diameter and 1 in/2.5 cm tall, spacing them fairly close together as they will not spread

much during baking. Using a fingertip dipped in cold water, smooth the peaks down to make rounded domes. On the remaining pan, using the remaining meringue, pipe out about four dozen "stems" about ¾ in/ 2 cm in diameter and 1 in/2.5 cm tall. Do not tamp down the peaks of the stems.

5. Bake until the meringues are crisp and set and release easily when lifted from the paper, about 1 hour. (Don't open the oven door for the first 45 minutes of the baking time, or the mushroom caps might crack.) Turn off the oven and let the meringues cool in the oven, with the door ajar, for at least 1 hour or up to 12 hours.

6. Remove the caps and stems from the pans. Using the tip of a small, sharp knife, make a small hole in the bottom of each cap. One at a time, spread the flat side of the cap with ganache, covering the hole. Insert the peak of the stem in the hole. Set aside to dry. Meringues can be stored in an airtight container at room temperature for up to 5 days.

7. Just before serving, sift cocoa over the caps.

THE MODEL BAKERY COOKBOOK

THE MODEL BAKERY ON COOKIES

Great cookies cannot be baked on flimsy baking sheets. Use sturdy, heavy-gauge half-sheet pans measuring about 18 by 13 in/46 by 33 cm, which have many advantages over smaller, thinner sheets. First of all, they just hold more cookies, which speeds up the operation. This is especially important when baking our oversized drop cookies. They also soak up the oven heat for even baking, whereas shiny baking sheets reflect the heat and have hot spots.

Drop cookies will bake most evenly if the dough is shaped into equal mounds. Use a food-portion scoop (we use our old friend, the number-16 scoop with about a ¼-cup/60-ml capacity), spacing the mounds as directed in the recipe.

It is a good idea to bake a single sheet of cookies as a test run to establish how much they spread and the exact baking time in your oven. A minute or two in either direction can make the difference between a soft, chewy cookie and a crisp, crumbly one. Both are good, but you may have a preference.

Even when it's not a test run, for the best results, bake one sheet of cookies at a time on the center rack of the oven, to be sure the baking sheet doesn't get too close to a heat source and cause overbaking. However, it is more practical to bake two sheets of cookies at a time, and it can be done if the baking sheets' positions are switched halfway through baking. Position oven racks in the top third and center of the oven and preheat the oven. Bake the cookies for half of their estimated baking time. Switch the positions of the pans from top to bottom, and also rotate the pans from front to back, and continue baking until the cookies are the required state of doneness.

Line the baking sheets with parchment paper. Some bakers like silicone baking mats, but they insulate the sheets and can keep cookies from crisping. If you like silicone mats, be sure to wipe them clean with hot water after every use, as they can soak up butter from the cookies, which will eventually go rancid and give the mats an off aroma and flavor.

We love cookie jars, but the sad truth is they don't really keep cookies fresh. Store cookies at room temperature in metal or plastic airtight containers with the layers separated by wax or parchment paper. Do not store fundamentally different cookies (for example, spicy and plain, or crisp and soft) together in the same container, or they will pick up each other's flavors, and your crisp cookies may soften.

GINGERBREAD HOUSE TEMPLATE

50% SCALE

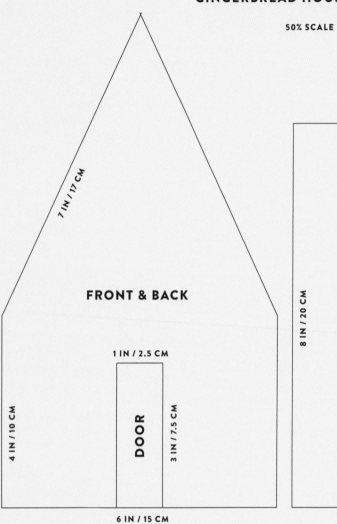

FRONT & BACK

7 IN / 17 CM

4 IN / 10 CM

1 IN / 2.5 CM

DOOR

3 IN / 7.5 CM

6 IN / 15 CM

7 IN / 17 CM

8 IN / 20 CM

ROOF

8 IN / 20 CM

3 IN / 7.5 CM

WINDOW

1 IN / 2.5 CM

4 IN / 10 CM

SIDE

RESOURCES

AMAZON.COM

www.amazon.com

You can purchase just about every baking item in this book from this super-supplier, from bread supplies (bannetons) and utensils (BeaterBlades and large rolling pins) to cake supplies (flat parchment paper and cardboard cake rounds and rectangles) and equipment (cake pans) to ingredients (Dutch-process cocoa, chocolate vermicelli, bulk almond paste, and organic flours).

CANDY WAREHOUSE

215 S. Douglas Street
El Segundo, CA 90245
(310) 343-4099
www.candywarehouse.com

Browse this site to become inspired by choices for decorating your gingerbread house.

KESTREL GROWTH BRANDS

PO Box 50042
Eugene, OR 97405
(888) 343-0002
www.kestrelgrowth.com

Kestrel Growth makes our favorite vanilla, Singing Dog.

KING ARTHUR FLOUR

135 Route 5 South
Norwich, VT 05055
(800) 827-6836
www.kingarthurflour.com

While King Arthur's line of flours is available nationally, you can also order from their excellent catalog or website, where you will also find a large selection of baking equipment and supplies.

THE PASTRY SAMPLER

Beach Cuisine
1672 Main Street, Suite E, no. 159
Ramona, CA 92065
(760) 440-9171
www.pastrysampler.com

An excellent array of everything you need for baking and decorating cakes, especially pastry tips.

WHOLE FOODS MARKETS

550 Bowie Street
Austin, TX 78703
(512) 477-4455
www.wholefoodsmarket.com

Cooks from all over the country shop at Whole Foods for organic flours, bulk chocolate, Dutch-process cocoa, and other baking supplies.

WILLIAMS-SONOMA

3250 Van Ness Avenue
San Francisco, CA 94109
(877) 812-6235
www.williams-sonoma.com

The nation's top kitchenware store has a carefully chosen selection of first-quality baking equipment.

ACKNOWLEDGMENTS

People often ask us about the secret to the Model Bakery's longevity—after all, thirty years is a long time. The answer is simple: Our bakery is more like a family than a business. Everyone's hard work allowed us to take the time we needed to write this book.

We have had many talented bakers and pastry chefs, without whom the bakery would be a very different place. These include Sandra Coltrin, Angela Gong, Melissa Biles, Raquel Bagatini, Chazz Mathemeier, Jen Emanuel, Linda King, and Veronica Villaneuva. Gordon Patty and our night bakers (indeed a tough shift) have our unconditional thanks and admiration. Alisha Williams, a beloved former employee, took time to help us test the cakes.

Our matchless, passionate bread-baking team, Isaac Cermak and Eli Colvin, are amazingly professional, knowledgeable, and hard working. They are dedicated to making the best bread in the Valley, and their commitment shows in every loaf.

St. Helena managers Chelsea Radcliffe and Emelie Poisson have expertise and management skills that belie their years. Customers think that Chelsea is a member of the Mitchell family (and in many ways, she is). Emelie is also a skilled baker, and has taken over the holiday cookie program so we rest assured that the next generation of pastry lovers will still have beautiful handmade cookies. Our wholesale manager at Oxbow, Tameeka Evans, holds it all together for our team. We owe many thanks for her dedication.

From the day we opened, the town of St. Helena welcomed us and helped us thrive. Margrit Mondavi and Virginia Van Asperen met every Saturday morning at the bakery, and helped spread the word; Molly Chappelet is a devoted customer who became a devoted friend. Priscilla Upton, Karen's partner in running the first catering business in the Napa Valley, established the quality assurance that has spread to the bakery. We were two cooks with no idea how to run a business who prospered due to hard work, good luck, and great friendships. Special thanks are also due to Isabel Mondavi, Sarah Forni, Janis Gay, and Caryl Knapp, among others, who helped us stage parties and serve at the local wineries.

We would also like to take this opportunity to thank the many dedicated bakers who worked with us through the years, especially Regina Mason, one of our first pastry chefs and a superb cake decorator. Thanks also to Rob Alexander, who revived our bread program and put us on the path to create our Oxbow bread division.

Our dear friends Peter and Christy Palmisano lent us their house as a test kitchen, with the same casual trust that someone else might lend you their favorite book. This ensured that the recipes worked in home ovens as well as they do in our brick ovens.

Special orders for wineries and restaurants have been a mainstay of our company. We are grateful to their support and friendship over the last three decades we have been in business. We are especially grateful to the Napa Valley Vintners who support our store almost daily. As we said before, Robert Mondavi Winery was there from the beginning, as was Joseph Phelps Vineyards (Karen cooked lunch there every Tuesday for many years). The crew at Spotswoode orders lunch many days of the week. The Harlan family, developers of the beautiful Meadowood resort, have supported us for many years. We are grateful to the farmers' markets in both St. Helena and Napa who have been customers for decades. And our old friends from the Baker's Dozen have inspired us with their professionalism (Carol Field, Flo Braker, Fran Gage, and Marion Cunningham), and to our loyal Valley customers who patronize our stores on a daily basis. Our bakery in the center of the Napa Valley is indeed fortunate. Thank you especially to Michael Chiarello, chef, owner of Bottega restaurant, and a longtime friend, for choosing our English muffins as "The Best Thing I Ever Ate," then featuring us on the Food Network program as his favorite local food. It was a marvelous honor that propelled our business to a new level. We are grateful for your support and friendship.

We are deeply grateful to our family for all of their love and support, which starts with two women who would be proud to see us baking every day. Karen's mother, Laurabelle, and her grandmother Stella, both set high standards in their kitchens that we still aspire to today.

THE MODEL BAKERY COOKBOOK

Husband and father, John Mitchell, has been devoted to our success from the beginning. He is as proud of our bakery as any of us here. A professional builder, he has done everything at the bakery from fixing tables and chairs to busing tables. We love you.

Sarah's son Alexander, who at seven has a highly advanced sense of taste, is a budding businessman with very impressive marketing skills. His little red head is well known around the Valley. He teaches us all something new every day. Sarah's husband, Chris Hansen, has supported the bakery especially with his technical computer skills and helped to develop our unique website. We thank him for his patience and love.

It was book producer Leslie Jonath who guided the project from Day One, along with our public relations team, Tom Fuller and Monty Sanders of Fuller and Sanders Communications. Leslie was a hard taskmaster, but we are told that is part of her job, which she did with charm and dedication. Her biggest contribution was introducing us to our co-writer Rick Rodgers. Without Rick, this book would never have happened! He took a hodgepodge of commercial recipes and transformed them into workable formulas for the home baker—no easy job. Rick is a true professional, who never let us cut corners or forget a step. Rick helped us turn years of baking into a real history and record of our past, something that Sarah had been asking Karen to do for decades. And now we have a friend for life!

Thank you to Frankie Frankeny, our talented photographer, for bringing her focus and artistic sense to our story. Kudos to prop stylist, Greg O'Connell, and food stylist, Nissa Quantstrum.

And last, but not least, we are thrilled to be published by Chronicle Books, which is known around the world for their beautiful work. Thank you to cookbook director Bill LeBlond, senior editor Amy Treadwell and senior designer Alice Chau, managing editors Doug Ogan and Marie Oishi, marketing manager Peter Perez, publicity manager David Hawk, and production coordinator Steve Kim.

Karen Mitchell
Sarah Mitchell

Peter and Christy Palmasino opened their beautiful home to Karen and me, and gave us a haven for creating this book. We worked very hard, but the load was lightened looking out on a vineyard from a farmhouse nested in the mountains above the Valley.

In my kitchen on the East Coast, the list begins, as always, with my dear kitchen manager Diane Kniss, who worked by my side to perfect the recipes after trial runs in Napa. My life partner, Patrick Fisher, never complained about being served another dish of fresh-plated English muffins. (Okay, who would?) Thanks also to Frank Mentesana, a cookbook writer and former bakery owner himself, for testing assistance. Amy Vogler assumed testing responsibilities at a crucial point, and I offer her a big bowl of gratitude with sprinkles on top.

Anne E. McBride, culinary program director of the Stragegic Initiatives Group at the Culinary Institute of America introduced me to master pastry chef Francisco Migoya, who was generous enough to answer some technical questions.

Leslie Jonath invited me to take part in this project. I will miss our early morning chats. Judith Dunham contributed to this book in many valuable ways.

I basked in the hospitality and friendship of the entire Mitchell family—Karen, John, and Sarah—and will always consider my time in Napa as a very special era.

It is a great pleasure to be reunited with Bill LeBlond, Peter Perez, Amy Treadwell, Doug Ogan, Marie Oishi, Alice Chau, David Hawk, and Steve Kim. I am especially thankful for the expertise of our copy editor, Deborah Kops, and for Amy's and Alice's patience and professionalism.

Rick Rodgers

INDEX